AF890193

This journal belongs to -

____

If found, contact me at:

____

Train Your Money Guided Journal

Train Your Money™ Guided Journal

Copyright © 2025 Janice Pierce

All rights reserved

Published by Achieve Financial Partners, LLC

Boise, ID, USA

No part of this publication may be copied, stored, or shared in any form without written permission from the author. It may not be lent, resold, or circulated in any format other than the one in which it was published, and photocopying for resale is not allowed.

This journal—part of *Sit, Buck, Sit – Part One of the Train Your Money™ series*—is created to guide and inspire your money journey. It's meant for educational and informational use only and should not replace advice from a financial, tax, or legal professional. The author and Achieve Financial Partners, LLC cannot be held responsible for actions taken based on its use. Please don't record account numbers, logins, or other sensitive details here, and remember to keep your journal stored safely.

I'm Glad You're Here!

You've taken the first step toward bringing calm and clarity to your money. Over the years, I've seen that when people get clear on their cash flow - what's coming in, what's going out, and what's truly important to them - they often discover **an extra $100-$200 a month** hiding in plain sight. That's money for savings, paying down debt, or simply breathing easier.

This journal is designed to guide you to clarity one page at a time. If you'd like extra guidance as you go, I've also created a companion course that walks you step by step through the same system. Whether you stick with the journal alone or pair it with the course, you're taking a powerful step toward financial confidence.

https://achievefinance.podia.com

What this journal will do for you

→ Give you a simple process you'll actually use - no apps, no formulas, just pen, paper and clarity.

→ Build your confidence around money - see where it's going without guilt or judgment.

→ Offer a calm, clear process to follow one month at a time.

→ Keep you motivated - fun prompts and reflections to connect money with your goals and values

This journal is about *progress, not perfection*. Start today and take the next step toward the life you want. Turn the page to see all the tools waiting for you inside.

Janice

Included in this Journal

- Quick-Start Checklist: How to Use This Journal
- The Four H's Change Wheel (beginning and end of journal)
- Monthly Trackers
    - Bill Tracker Calendar
    - Fixed Expenses Tracker
        - Housing, Transportation, Debt Minimums, Care Expenses
        - Emergency Savings Fund
        - Extra Debt Payments (counts as savings!)
    - Credit Card Spending Tracker
    - Refocus, Reflect & Notes Pages
- Weekly Tracker
    - Sneaky Spend Zones (food, shopping, entertainment)
- Quarterly (every 3 months) Tracker
    - Extra Debt Payments (counts as savings!)
- Fun & Informative Pages - to Make Money More Interesting
    - Fact Sheets
    - Subscription Tracker
    - Freeform Grid Pages for Ideas, Reflections or Journaling
    - Prompt Pages - Think, Act, Feel
- Extra Pages for Notes & Tracking

BUDGETING FUN FACTS

It takes about 90 days to get used to using a budget. Don't give up!

Having a budget can reduce financial stress and improve mental well-being by providing a sense of security and control

✔ Quick-Start Checklist: How to Use This Journal

→ **Set up the month:**

☐ Start with the current month, even if it's not the first of the month

☐ Write in **paydays** and **bill due dates** on the Bill Tracker Calendar

☐ Follow the instructions at the bottom of the Bill Tracker Calendar to see if there is money left over or if adjustments need to be made

→ **Track fixed expenses monthly:**

☐ Housing

☐ Transportation

☐ Debt minimums (the amount needed to stay current)

☐ Care expenses (kids, pets, health, etc.)

→ **Track flexible expenses weekly:**

☐ Food, Shopping, Entertainment

☐ Savings & extra debt payments (these count as **savings**)

→ **Refocus, Reflect & Write:**

☐ Write thoughts, ideas and goals on the pages provided at the end of each month

☐ Consistent, small steps create large changes

☐ Focus on one month at a time and change will happen

→ **Pro Tips:**

☐ Tracking expenses weekly - spot patterns sooner and adjust faster

☐ Do not write account numbers or login information in your journal

☐ **Progress > perfection**. Take one small step each day

The Four H's Change Wheel

rate yourself 1 (least confident) to 10 (most confident) in each area

HANDS- *MONEY BEHAVIORS*

HEAD - *FINANCIAL KNOWLEDGE*

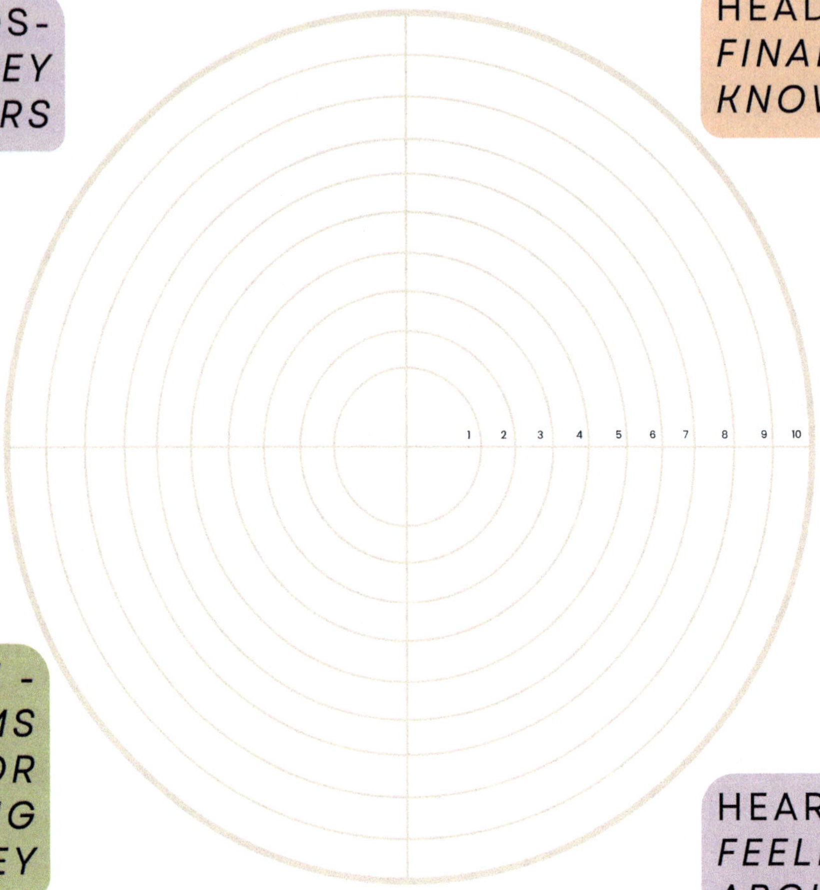

HOW - *SYSTEMS FOR TRACKING MONEY*

HEART - *FEELINGS ABOUT MONEY*

"A starting point to guide your next steps and measure your growth."

I'M STARTING WITH...

____

____

____

____

____

____

Bill Tracker Calendar

Month: ____________________

Monday	Tuesday	Wednesday	Thursday	Friday	Saturday	Sunday	Amount Left over
☐	☐	☐	☐	☐	☐	☐	
☐	☐	☐	☐	☐	☐	☐	
☐	☐	☐	☐	☐	☐	☐	
☐	☐	☐	☐	☐	☐	☐	
☐	☐	☐	☐	☐	☐	☐	

Instructions

1. Enter take-home pay on pay dates
2. Enter bills on due dates
3. Enter other expenses for this month – insurance, holidays, gifts
4. Track left over amount each week
5. Carry over to next week if positive
6. If negative, use money from another category

MONEY
BUCKET
Approach
Train Your Money™
INCOME
FIXED EXPENSES
FLEXIBLE EXPENSES
SAVINGS

🐾 Train Your Spending with the Money Bucket Plan

Simple. Flexible. Built for real life.

The **percentage spending plan** is a perennial favorite plan because it works for any income level. Just split your take-home pay into 3 easy buckets:

The Classic 50/30/20 Plan

- **50% Needs** - Rent, utilities, groceries, insurance, transportation
- **30% Wants** - Dining out, fun, shopping, hobbies
- **20% Savings** - Emergency fund, debt payoff, retirement, future goals

---

The Real-Life 70/20/10 Plan

For one-income households, lower wages, or high cost-of-living areas:

- **70% Needs** - Covers the basics without the guilt
- **20% Wants** - Still room for joy
- **10% Savings** - Small steps still build the future

Buck's Tip:

"Don't stress the perfect split - just give every dollar a job and keep it moving toward your goals!"

Pick Your Plan. Track Your Spending. Adjust as Needed.

No matter which plan you choose, the goal is progress—not perfection.
The more awareness you have, the more *you* control your money (not the other way around).

Monthly Bill Tracker

MONTH ______________________

Fixed - The expenses that don't change from month to month

Fluctuates - Expenses that change from month to month

NET INCOME ______________________

HOUSING

Date	Who Did You Pay	Amount	Fixed	Fluctuates	Account Paid From	Payment Method (Auto, Debit, Credit)	Still Owe? How much? (Balance)
		$	☐	☐			
		$	☐	☐			
		$	☐	☐			
		$	☐	☐			
		$	☐	☐			
		$	☐	☐			
		$	☐	☐			
		$	☐	☐			
		$	☐	☐			
		$	☐	☐			
		$	☐	☐			
		$	☐	☐			
		$	☐	☐			
		$	☐	☐			
	TOTAL						

> This page is where the magic starts - but it can feel intimidating the first time. In the Train Your Money™ Course, we fill this out together, step by step, with real examples so you know exactly how to make it work for you.

What did you learn about your fixed and fluctating housing spending? ______________________

Where can your money work better for you? ______________________

More efficient money = more for what matters!

TRANSPORTATION

Date	Who Did You Pay	Amount	Fixed	Fluctuates	Account Paid From	Payment Method (Auto, Debit, Credit)	Still Owe? How much? (Balance)
		$	☐	☐			
		$	☐	☐			
		$	☐	☐			
		$	☐	☐			
		$	☐	☐			
		$	☐	☐			
		$	☐	☐			
		$	☐	☐			
		$	☐	☐			
		$	☐	☐			
		$	☐	☐			
		$	☐	☐			
	TOTAL						

What did you learn about your fixed and fluctating transportation spending? ______________________

Where can your money work better for you? ______________________

More efficient money = more for what matters!

Monthly Bill Tracker

MONTH ____________________

Fixed - The expenses that don't change from month to month

Fluctuates - Expenses that change from month to month

NET INCOME ____________________

DEBT MINIMUMS - What is needed to keep the debt current

Date	Who Did You Pay	Amount	Fixed	Fluctuates	Account Paid From	Payment Method (Auto, Debit, Credit)	Still Owe? How much? (Balance)
		$	☐	☐			
		$	☐	☐			
		$	☐	☐			
		$	☐	☐			
		$	☐	☐			
		$	☐	☐			
		$	☐	☐			
		$	☐	☐			
		$	☐	☐			
		$	☐	☐			
		$	☐	☐			
		$	☐	☐			
		$	☐	☐			
		$	☐	☐			
	TOTAL						

What did you learn about your fixed and fluctating debt spending? ____________________

Where can your money work better for you? ____________________

More efficient money = more for what matters!

CARE EXPENSES - Personal, Children, Pets

Date	Who Did You Pay	Amount	Fixed	Fluctuates	Account Paid From	Payment Method (Auto, Debit, Credit)	Still Owe? How much? (Balance)
		$	☐	☐			
		$	☐	☐			
		$	☐	☐			
		$	☐	☐			
		$	☐	☐			
		$	☐	☐			
		$	☐	☐			
		$	☐	☐			
		$	☐	☐			
		$	☐	☐			
		$	☐	☐			
		$	☐	☐			
		$	☐	☐			
	TOTAL						

What did you learn about your fixed and fluctating care spending? ____________________

Where can your money work better for you? ____________________

More efficient money = more for what matters!

Your Sneaky Spend Zones

Month________________

Week (circle) 1 2 3 4 5

Food, shopping, and entertainment are the top categories for mindless overspending

Track these weekly (plus any others you think might be draining your money bucket) and see how much more you keep by month's end!

FOOD			SHOPPING			ENTERTAINMENT		
Amount $	Debit*	Credit*	Amount $	Debit	Credit	Amount $	Debit	Credit
______	☐	☐	______	☐	☐	______	☐	☐
______	☐	☐	______	☐	☐	______	☐	☐
______	☐	☐	______	☐	☐	______	☐	☐
______	☐	☐	______	☐	☐	______	☐	☐
______	☐	☐	______	☐	☐	______	☐	☐
______	☐	☐	______	☐	☐	______	☐	☐
______	☐	☐	______	☐	☐	______	☐	☐
______	☐	☐	______	☐	☐	______	☐	☐
______	☐	☐	______	☐	☐	______	☐	☐
______	☐	☐	______	☐	☐	______	☐	☐
Total ______			Total ______			Total ______		

*Debit - Money comes out of your account right away (checking or savings) when you spend it.
*Credit - Purchases add to a running balance you must pay off by the due date to avoid interest.

Your Sneaky Spend Zones

Month__________________

Week (circle) 1 2 3 4 5

Food, shopping, and entertainment are the top categories for mindless overspending

Track these weekly (plus any others you think might be draining your money bucket) and see how much more you keep by month's end!

FOOD			SHOPPING			ENTERTAINMENT		
Amount $	Debit*	Credit*	Amount $	Debit	Credit	Amount $	Debit	Credit
________	☐	☐	________	☐	☐	________	☐	☐
________	☐	☐	________	☐	☐	________	☐	☐
________	☐	☐	________	☐	☐	________	☐	☐
________	☐	☐	________	☐	☐	________	☐	☐
________	☐	☐	________	☐	☐	________	☐	☐
________	☐	☐	________	☐	☐	________	☐	☐
________	☐	☐	________	☐	☐	________	☐	☐
________	☐	☐	________	☐	☐	________	☐	☐
________	☐	☐	________	☐	☐	________	☐	☐
________	☐	☐	________	☐	☐	________	☐	☐

Total ________ Total ________ Total ________

*Debit - Money comes out of your account right away (checking or savings) when you spend it.
*Credit - Purchases add to a running balance you must pay off by the due date to avoid interest.

Your Sneaky Spend Zones

Month__________________

Week (circle) 1 2 3 4 5

Food, shopping, and entertainment are the top categories for mindless overspending

Track these weekly (plus any others you think might be draining your money bucket) and see how much more you keep by month's end!

FOOD			SHOPPING			ENTERTAINMENT		
Amount $	Debit*	Credit*	Amount $	Debit	Credit	Amount $	Debit	Credit
________	☐	☐	________	☐	☐	________	☐	☐
________	☐	☐	________	☐	☐	________	☐	☐
________	☐	☐	________	☐	☐	________	☐	☐
________	☐	☐	________	☐	☐	________	☐	☐
________	☐	☐	________	☐	☐	________	☐	☐
________	☐	☐	________	☐	☐	________	☐	☐
________	☐	☐	________	☐	☐	________	☐	☐
________	☐	☐	________	☐	☐	________	☐	☐
________	☐	☐	________	☐	☐	________	☐	☐
________	☐	☐	________	☐	☐	________	☐	☐
Total ________			Total ________			Total ________		

*Debit - Money comes out of your account right away (checking or savings) when you spend it.
*Credit - Purchases add to a running balance you must pay off by the due date to avoid interest.

Your Sneaky Spend Zones

Month________________

Week (circle) 1 2 3 4 5

Food, shopping, and entertainment are the top categories for mindless overspending

Track these weekly (plus any others you think might be draining your money bucket) and see how much more you keep by month's end!

FOOD			**SHOPPING**			**ENTERTAINMENT**		
Amount $	Debit*	Credit*	Amount $	Debit	Credit	Amount $	Debit	Credit
______	☐	☐	______	☐	☐	______	☐	☐
______	☐	☐	______	☐	☐	______	☐	☐
______	☐	☐	______	☐	☐	______	☐	☐
______	☐	☐	______	☐	☐	______	☐	☐
______	☐	☐	______	☐	☐	______	☐	☐
______	☐	☐	______	☐	☐	______	☐	☐
______	☐	☐	______	☐	☐	______	☐	☐
______	☐	☐	______	☐	☐	______	☐	☐
______	☐	☐	______	☐	☐	______	☐	☐
______	☐	☐	______	☐	☐	______	☐	☐
Total ______			Total ______			Total ______		

*Debit - Money comes out of your account right away (checking or savings) when you spend it.
*Credit - Purchases add to a running balance you must pay off by the due date to avoid interest.

Credit Card Spending Tracker

Spend, Pay, Repeat

Payment Date	Card Name	Charged	Paid	Balance Up or Down

Fixed Repayment Loan

Include all: personal loans, tax loans, student loan, medical loans, auto loans

Creditor	Balance	Minimum Payment	Interest Rate

Debt

Installment

Installment Loan - borrow once and repay over time in fixed monthly payments.

Revolving

Revolving Credit - lets you borrow, repay, and borrow again up to a set limit.

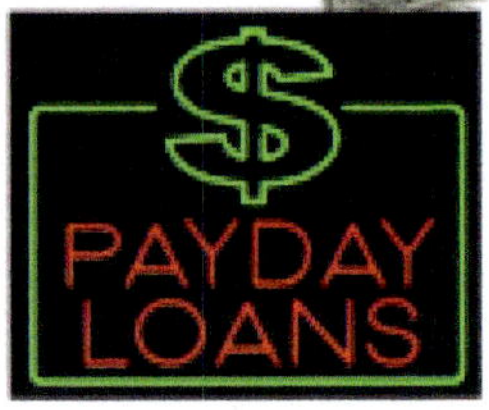

https://achievefinance.podia.com

Want to feel confident—not confused—about debt?

Learn how to use credit wisely, ditch high-interest debt, and build a strong financial foundation.

*Sign up for the **Debt & Credit Course** at Train Your Money™ and start turning debt into a tool, not a trap.*

Subscription Tracker

Subscription	Cost	Payment Method	Monthly/ Annual	Due Date	Auto Renew	Notes
			M A			
			M A			
			M A			
			M A			
			M A			
			M A			
			M A			
			M A			
			M A			
			M A			
			M A			
			M A			
			M A			
			M A			
			M A			
			M A			
			M A			
			M A			
			M A			

Refocus, Reflect + Notes

Use this space to capture your thoughts, goals or aha moments:

"If you think you are too small to make a difference, try sleeping in a room with a mosquito."

Dalai Lama

https://achievefinance.podia.com

Bill Tracker Calendar

Month: ____________________

Monday	Tuesday	Wednesday	Thursday	Friday	Saturday	Sunday	Amount Left over
☐	☐	☐	☐	☐	☐	☐	
☐	☐	☐	☐	☐	☐	☐	
☐	☐	☐	☐	☐	☐	☐	
☐	☐	☐	☐	☐	☐	☐	
☐	☐	☐	☐	☐	☐	☐	

Instructions

1. Enter take-home pay on pay dates
2. Enter bills on due dates
3. Enter other expenses for this month – insurance, holidays, gifts
4. Track left over amount each week
5. Carry over to next week if positive
6. If negative, use money from another category

Monthly Bill Tracker

MONTH ______________________

Fixed - The expenses that don't change from month to month

Fluctuates - Expenses that change from month to month

NET INCOME ___________________

HOUSING

Date	Who Did You Pay	Amount	Fixed	Fluctuates	Account Paid From	Payment Method (Auto, Debit, Credit)	Still Owe? How much? (Balance)
		$	☐	☐			
		$	☐	☐			
		$	☐	☐			
		$	☐	☐			
		$	☐	☐			
		$	☐	☐			
		$	☐	☐			
		$	☐	☐			
		$	☐	☐			
		$	☐	☐			
		$	☐	☐			
		$	☐	☐			
		$	☐	☐			
		$	☐	☐			
	TOTAL						

What did you learn about your fixed and fluctating housing spending? ____________

Where can your money work better for you? ____________

More efficient money = more for what matters!

TRANSPORTATION

Date	Who Did You Pay	Amount	Fixed	Fluctuates	Account Paid From	Payment Method (Auto, Debit, Credit)	Still Owe? How much? (Balance)
		$	☐	☐			
		$	☐	☐			
		$	☐	☐			
		$	☐	☐			
		$	☐	☐			
		$	☐	☐			
		$	☐	☐			
		$	☐	☐			
		$	☐	☐			
		$	☐	☐			
		$	☐	☐			
		$	☐	☐			
	TOTAL						

What did you learn about your fixed and fluctating transportation spending? ____________

Where can your money work better for you? ____________

More efficient money = more for what matters!

Monthly Bill Tracker

MONTH ______________________

Fixed - The expenses that don't change from month to month

Fluctuates - Expenses that change from month to month

NET INCOME ___________________

DEBT MINIMUMS - What is needed to keep the debt current

Date	Who Did You Pay	Amount	Fixed	Fluctuates	Account Paid From	Payment Method (Auto, Debit, Credit)	Still Owe? How much? (Balance)
		$	☐	☐			
		$	☐	☐			
		$	☐	☐			
		$	☐	☐			
		$	☐	☐			
		$	☐	☐			
		$	☐	☐			
		$	☐	☐			
		$	☐	☐			
		$	☐	☐			
		$	☐	☐			
		$	☐	☐			
		$	☐	☐			
		$	☐	☐			
	TOTAL	________					

What did you learn about your fixed and fluctating debt spending? ____________________

Where can your money work better for you? ____________________

More efficient money = more for what matters!

CARE EXPENSES - Personal, Children, Pets

Date	Who Did You Pay	Amount	Fixed	Fluctuates	Account Paid From	Payment Method (Auto, Debit, Credit)	Still Owe? How much? (Balance)
		$	☐	☐			
		$	☐	☐			
		$	☐	☐			
		$	☐	☐			
		$	☐	☐			
		$	☐	☐			
		$	☐	☐			
		$	☐	☐			
		$	☐	☐			
		$	☐	☐			
		$	☐	☐			
		$	☐	☐			
		$	☐	☐			
	TOTAL	________					

What did you learn about your fixed and fluctating care spending? ____________________

Where can your money work better for you? ____________________

More efficient money = more for what matters!

Your Sneaky Spend Zones

Month ________________

Week (circle) 1 2 3 4 5

Food, shopping, and entertainment are the top categories for mindless overspending

Track these weekly (plus any others you think might be draining your money bucket) and see how much more you keep by month's end!

FOOD			SHOPPING			ENTERTAINMENT		
Amount $	Debit*	Credit*	Amount $	Debit	Credit	Amount $	Debit	Credit
______	☐	☐	______	☐	☐	______	☐	☐
______	☐	☐	______	☐	☐	______	☐	☐
______	☐	☐	______	☐	☐	______	☐	☐
______	☐	☐	______	☐	☐	______	☐	☐
______	☐	☐	______	☐	☐	______	☐	☐
______	☐	☐	______	☐	☐	______	☐	☐
______	☐	☐	______	☐	☐	______	☐	☐
______	☐	☐	______	☐	☐	______	☐	☐
______	☐	☐	______	☐	☐	______	☐	☐
______	☐	☐	______	☐	☐	______	☐	☐
Total ______			Total ______			Total ______		

*Debit - Money comes out of your account right away (checking or savings) when you spend it.
*Credit - Purchases add to a running balance you must pay off by the due date to avoid interest.

Your Sneaky Spend Zones

Month________________

Week (circle) 1 2 3 4 5

Food, shopping, and entertainment are the top categories for mindless overspending

Track these weekly (plus any others you think might be draining your money bucket) and see how much more you keep by month's end!

FOOD			SHOPPING			ENTERTAINMENT		
Amount $	Debit*	Credit*	Amount $	Debit	Credit	Amount $	Debit	Credit
______	☐	☐	______	☐	☐	______	☐	☐
______	☐	☐	______	☐	☐	______	☐	☐
______	☐	☐	______	☐	☐	______	☐	☐
______	☐	☐	______	☐	☐	______	☐	☐
______	☐	☐	______	☐	☐	______	☐	☐
______	☐	☐	______	☐	☐	______	☐	☐
______	☐	☐	______	☐	☐	______	☐	☐
______	☐	☐	______	☐	☐	______	☐	☐
______	☐	☐	______	☐	☐	______	☐	☐
______	☐	☐	______	☐	☐	______	☐	☐

Total ________ Total ________ Total ________

*Debit - Money comes out of your account right away (checking or savings) when you spend it.
*Credit - Purchases add to a running balance you must pay off by the due date to avoid interest.

Your Sneaky Spend Zones

Month ________________

Week (circle) 1 2 3 4 5

Food, shopping, and entertainment are the top categories for mindless overspending

Track these weekly (plus any others you think might be draining your money bucket) and see how much more you keep by month's end!

FOOD			SHOPPING			ENTERTAINMENT		
Amount $	Debit*	Credit*	Amount $	Debit	Credit	Amount $	Debit	Credit
______	☐	☐	______	☐	☐	______	☐	☐
______	☐	☐	______	☐	☐	______	☐	☐
______	☐	☐	______	☐	☐	______	☐	☐
______	☐	☐	______	☐	☐	______	☐	☐
______	☐	☐	______	☐	☐	______	☐	☐
______	☐	☐	______	☐	☐	______	☐	☐
______	☐	☐	______	☐	☐	______	☐	☐
______	☐	☐	______	☐	☐	______	☐	☐
______	☐	☐	______	☐	☐	______	☐	☐
______	☐	☐	______	☐	☐	______	☐	☐
Total ______			Total ______			Total ______		

*Debit - Money comes out of your account right away (checking or savings) when you spend it.
*Credit - Purchases add to a running balance you must pay off by the due date to avoid interest.

Your Sneaky Spend Zones

Month________________

Week (circle) 1 2 3 4 5

Food, shopping, and entertainment are the top categories for mindless overspending

Track these weekly (plus any others you think might be draining your money bucket) and see how much more you keep by month's end!

FOOD			**SHOPPING**			**ENTERTAINMENT**		
Amount $	Debit*	Credit*	Amount $	Debit	Credit	Amount $	Debit	Credit
______	☐	☐	______	☐	☐	______	☐	☐
______	☐	☐	______	☐	☐	______	☐	☐
______	☐	☐	______	☐	☐	______	☐	☐
______	☐	☐	______	☐	☐	______	☐	☐
______	☐	☐	______	☐	☐	______	☐	☐
______	☐	☐	______	☐	☐	______	☐	☐
______	☐	☐	______	☐	☐	______	☐	☐
______	☐	☐	______	☐	☐	______	☐	☐
______	☐	☐	______	☐	☐	______	☐	☐
______	☐	☐	______	☐	☐	______	☐	☐
Total ______			Total ______			Total ______		

*Debit - Money comes out of your account right away (checking or savings) when you spend it.
*Credit - Purchases add to a running balance you must pay off by the due date to avoid interest.

Credit Card Spending Tracker

Spend, Pay, Repeat

Payment Date	Card Name	Charged	Paid	Balance Up or Down

NOTES

Money Matters: Piece by Piece

Stack your savings, tame your spending, crush your debt, and level up your credit—one puzzle piece at a time

Bill Tracker Calendar

Month: ____________________

Monday	Tuesday	Wednesday	Thursday	Friday	Saturday	Sunday	Amount Left over
☐	☐	☐	☐	☐	☐	☐	
☐	☐	☐	☐	☐	☐	☐	
☐	☐	☐	☐	☐	☐	☐	
☐	☐	☐	☐	☐	☐	☐	
☐	☐	☐	☐	☐	☐	☐	

Instructions

1. Enter take-home pay on pay dates
2. Enter bills on due dates
3. Enter other expenses for this month – insurance, holidays, gifts
4. Track left over amount each week
5. Carry over to next week if positive
6. If negative, use money from another category

Monthly Bill Tracker

MONTH ____________________

Fixed - The expenses that don't change from month to month

Fluctuates - Expenses that change from month to month

NET INCOME ____________________

HOUSING

Date	Who Did You Pay	Amount	Fixed	Fluctuates	Account Paid From	Payment Method (Auto, Debit, Credit)	Still Owe? How much? (Balance)
		$	☐	☐			
		$	☐	☐			
		$	☐	☐			
		$	☐	☐			
		$	☐	☐			
		$	☐	☐			
		$	☐	☐			
		$	☐	☐			
		$	☐	☐			
		$	☐	☐			
		$	☐	☐			
		$	☐	☐			
		$	☐	☐			
		$	☐	☐			
	TOTAL	______					

What did you learn about your fixed and fluctating housing spending? ____________________

Where can your money work better for you? ____________________

More efficient money = more for what matters!

TRANSPORTATION

Date	Who Did You Pay	Amount	Fixed	Fluctuates	Account Paid From	Payment Method (Auto, Debit, Credit)	Still Owe? How much? (Balance)
		$	☐	☐			
		$	☐	☐			
		$	☐	☐			
		$	☐	☐			
		$	☐	☐			
		$	☐	☐			
		$	☐	☐			
		$	☐	☐			
		$	☐	☐			
		$	☐	☐			
		$	☐	☐			
		$	☐	☐			
	TOTAL	______					

What did you learn about your fixed and fluctating transportation spending? ____________________

Where can your money work better for you? ____________________

More efficient money = more for what matters!

Monthly Bill Tracker

MONTH ____________________

Fixed - The expenses that don't change from month to month

Fluctuates - Expenses that change from month to month

NET INCOME ____________________

DEBT MINIMUMS - What is needed to keep the debt current

Date	Who Did You Pay	Amount	Fixed	Fluctuates	Account Paid From	Payment Method (Auto, Debit, Credit)	Still Owe? How much? (Balance)
		$	☐	☐			
		$	☐	☐			
		$	☐	☐			
		$	☐	☐			
		$	☐	☐			
		$	☐	☐			
		$	☐	☐			
		$	☐	☐			
		$	☐	☐			
		$	☐	☐			
		$	☐	☐			
		$	☐	☐			
		$	☐	☐			
		$	☐	☐			
	TOTAL						

What did you learn about your fixed and fluctating debt spending? ____________________

Where can your money work better for you? ____________________

More efficient money = more for what matters!

CARE EXPENSES - Personal, Children, Pets

Date	Who Did You Pay	Amount	Fixed	Fluctuates	Account Paid From	Payment Method (Auto, Debit, Credit)	Still Owe? How much? (Balance)
		$	☐	☐			
		$	☐	☐			
		$	☐	☐			
		$	☐	☐			
		$	☐	☐			
		$	☐	☐			
		$	☐	☐			
		$	☐	☐			
		$	☐	☐			
		$	☐	☐			
		$	☐	☐			
		$	☐	☐			
		$	☐	☐			
	TOTAL						

What did you learn about your fixed and fluctating care spending? ____________________

Where can your money work better for you? ____________________

More efficient money = more for what matters!

Your Sneaky Spend Zones

Month________________

Week (circle) 1 2 3 4 5

Food, shopping, and entertainment are the top categories for mindless overspending

Track these weekly (plus any others you think might be draining your money bucket) and see how much more you keep by month's end!

FOOD			SHOPPING			ENTERTAINMENT		
Amount $	Debit*	Credit*	Amount $	Debit	Credit	Amount $	Debit	Credit
______	☐	☐	______	☐	☐	______	☐	☐
______	☐	☐	______	☐	☐	______	☐	☐
______	☐	☐	______	☐	☐	______	☐	☐
______	☐	☐	______	☐	☐	______	☐	☐
______	☐	☐	______	☐	☐	______	☐	☐
______	☐	☐	______	☐	☐	______	☐	☐
______	☐	☐	______	☐	☐	______	☐	☐
______	☐	☐	______	☐	☐	______	☐	☐
______	☐	☐	______	☐	☐	______	☐	☐
______	☐	☐	______	☐	☐	______	☐	☐
Total ______			Total ______			Total ______		

*Debit - Money comes out of your account right away (checking or savings) when you spend it.
*Credit - Purchases add to a running balance you must pay off by the due date to avoid interest.

Your Sneaky Spend Zones

Month________________

Week (circle) 1 2 3 4 5

Food, shopping, and entertainment are the top categories for mindless overspending

Track these weekly (plus any others you think might be draining your money bucket) and see how much more you keep by month's end!

FOOD			SHOPPING			ENTERTAINMENT		
Amount $	Debit*	Credit*	Amount $	Debit	Credit	Amount $	Debit	Credit
______	☐	☐	______	☐	☐	______	☐	☐
______	☐	☐	______	☐	☐	______	☐	☐
______	☐	☐	______	☐	☐	______	☐	☐
______	☐	☐	______	☐	☐	______	☐	☐
______	☐	☐	______	☐	☐	______	☐	☐
______	☐	☐	______	☐	☐	______	☐	☐
______	☐	☐	______	☐	☐	______	☐	☐
______	☐	☐	______	☐	☐	______	☐	☐
______	☐	☐	______	☐	☐	______	☐	☐
______	☐	☐	______	☐	☐	______	☐	☐

Total ________ Total ________ Total ________

*Debit - Money comes out of your account right away (checking or savings) when you spend it.
*Credit - Purchases add to a running balance you must pay off by the due date to avoid interest.

Your Sneaky Spend Zones

Month________________

Week (circle) 1 2 3 4 5

Food, shopping, and entertainment are the top categories for mindless overspending

Track these weekly (plus any others you think might be draining your money bucket) and see how much more you keep by month's end!

FOOD			SHOPPING			ENTERTAINMENT		
Amount $	Debit*	Credit*	Amount $	Debit	Credit	Amount $	Debit	Credit
______	☐	☐	______	☐	☐	______	☐	☐
______	☐	☐	______	☐	☐	______	☐	☐
______	☐	☐	______	☐	☐	______	☐	☐
______	☐	☐	______	☐	☐	______	☐	☐
______	☐	☐	______	☐	☐	______	☐	☐
______	☐	☐	______	☐	☐	______	☐	☐
______	☐	☐	______	☐	☐	______	☐	☐
______	☐	☐	______	☐	☐	______	☐	☐
______	☐	☐	______	☐	☐	______	☐	☐
______	☐	☐	______	☐	☐	______	☐	☐
Total ______			Total ______			Total ______		

*Debit - Money comes out of your account right away (checking or savings) when you spend it.
*Credit - Purchases add to a running balance you must pay off by the due date to avoid interest.

Your Sneaky Spend Zones

Month________________

Week (circle) 1 2 3 4 5

Food, shopping, and entertainment are the top categories for mindless overspending

Track these weekly (plus any others you think might be draining your money bucket) and see how much more you keep by month's end!

FOOD			SHOPPING			ENTERTAINMENT		
Amount $	Debit*	Credit*	Amount $	Debit	Credit	Amount $	Debit	Credit
________	☐	☐	________	☐	☐	________	☐	☐
________	☐	☐	________	☐	☐	________	☐	☐
________	☐	☐	________	☐	☐	________	☐	☐
________	☐	☐	________	☐	☐	________	☐	☐
________	☐	☐	________	☐	☐	________	☐	☐
________	☐	☐	________	☐	☐	________	☐	☐
________	☐	☐	________	☐	☐	________	☐	☐
________	☐	☐	________	☐	☐	________	☐	☐
________	☐	☐	________	☐	☐	________	☐	☐
________	☐	☐	________	☐	☐	________	☐	☐
Total ________			Total ________			Total ________		

*Debit - Money comes out of your account right away (checking or savings) when you spend it.
*Credit - Purchases add to a running balance you must pay off by the due date to avoid interest.

Credit Card Spending Tracker

Spend, Pay, Repeat

Payment Date	Card Name	Charged	Paid	Balance Up or Down

NOTES

Dear Future Me

ABOUT THIS LETTER:

Take a moment to write a letter to your future self-someone who's one year further along in your financial journey. A lot can change in a year. This letter is your reminder that progress is possible, even one small step at a time.

- What habits will you be proud of?
- What challenges have you overcome?
- What does life feel like now that money isn't as stressful?

Refocus, Reflect + Notes

Use this space to capture your thoughts, goals or aha moments:

"Money is only a tool. It will take you wherever you wish, but it will not replace you as the driver."

Ayn Rand

https://achievefinance.podia.com

Bill Tracker Calendar

Month: ____________________

Monday	Tuesday	Wednesday	Thursday	Friday	Saturday	Sunday	Amount Left over
☐	☐	☐	☐	☐	☐	☐	
☐	☐	☐	☐	☐	☐	☐	
☐	☐	☐	☐	☐	☐	☐	
☐	☐	☐	☐	☐	☐	☐	
☐	☐	☐	☐	☐	☐	☐	

Instructions

1. Enter take-home pay on pay dates
2. Enter bills on due dates
3. Enter other expenses for this month – insurance, holidays, gifts
4. Track left over amount each week
5. Carry over to next week if positive
6. If negative, use money from another category

Monthly Bill Tracker

MONTH ____________________

Fixed - The expenses that don't change from month to month

Fluctuates - Expenses that change from month to month

NET INCOME ____________________

HOUSING

Date	Who Did You Pay	Amount	Fixed	Fluctuates	Account Paid From	Payment Method (Auto, Debit, Credit)	Still Owe? How much? (Balance)
		$	☐	☐			
		$	☐	☐			
		$	☐	☐			
		$	☐	☐			
		$	☐	☐			
		$	☐	☐			
		$	☐	☐			
		$	☐	☐			
		$	☐	☐			
		$	☐	☐			
		$	☐	☐			
		$	☐	☐			
		$	☐	☐			
		$	☐	☐			
	TOTAL	______					

What did you learn about your fixed and fluctating housing spending? ____________________

Where can your money work better for you? ____________________

More efficient money = more for what matters!

TRANSPORTATION

Date	Who Did You Pay	Amount	Fixed	Fluctuates	Account Paid From	Payment Method (Auto, Debit, Credit)	Still Owe? How much? (Balance)
		$	☐	☐			
		$	☐	☐			
		$	☐	☐			
		$	☐	☐			
		$	☐	☐			
		$	☐	☐			
		$	☐	☐			
		$	☐	☐			
		$	☐	☐			
		$	☐	☐			
		$	☐	☐			
		$	☐	☐			
	TOTAL	______					

What did you learn about your fixed and fluctating transportation spending? ____________________

Where can your money work better for you? ____________________

More efficient money = more for what matters!

Monthly Bill Tracker

MONTH ______________________

Fixed - The expenses that don't change from month to month

Fluctuates - Expenses that change from month to month

NET INCOME ____________________

DEBT MINIMUMS - What is needed to keep the debt current

Date	Who Did You Pay	Amount	Fixed	Fluctuates	Account Paid From	Payment Method (Auto, Debit, Credit)	Still Owe? How much? (Balance)
		$	☐	☐			
		$	☐	☐			
		$	☐	☐			
		$	☐	☐			
		$	☐	☐			
		$	☐	☐			
		$	☐	☐			
		$	☐	☐			
		$	☐	☐			
		$	☐	☐			
		$	☐	☐			
		$	☐	☐			
		$	☐	☐			
		$	☐	☐			
	TOTAL						

What did you learn about your fixed and fluctating debt spending? ____________________

Where can your money work better for you? ____________________

More efficient money = more for what matters!

CARE EXPENSES - Personal, Children, Pets

Date	Who Did You Pay	Amount	Fixed	Fluctuates	Account Paid From	Payment Method (Auto, Debit, Credit)	Still Owe? How much? (Balance)
		$	☐	☐			
		$	☐	☐			
		$	☐	☐			
		$	☐	☐			
		$	☐	☐			
		$	☐	☐			
		$	☐	☐			
		$	☐	☐			
		$	☐	☐			
		$	☐	☐			
		$	☐	☐			
		$	☐	☐			
		$	☐	☐			
	TOTAL						

What did you learn about your fixed and fluctating care spending? ____________________

Where can your money work better for you? ____________________

More efficient money = more for what matters!

Your Sneaky Spend Zones

Month________________

Week (circle) 1 2 3 4 5

Food, shopping, and entertainment are the top categories for mindless overspending

Track these weekly (plus any others you think might be draining your money bucket) and see how much more you keep by month's end!

FOOD			**SHOPPING**			**ENTERTAINMENT**		
Amount $	Debit*	Credit*	Amount $	Debit	Credit	Amount $	Debit	Credit
_______	☐	☐	_______	☐	☐	_______	☐	☐
_______	☐	☐	_______	☐	☐	_______	☐	☐
_______	☐	☐	_______	☐	☐	_______	☐	☐
_______	☐	☐	_______	☐	☐	_______	☐	☐
_______	☐	☐	_______	☐	☐	_______	☐	☐
_______	☐	☐	_______	☐	☐	_______	☐	☐
_______	☐	☐	_______	☐	☐	_______	☐	☐
_______	☐	☐	_______	☐	☐	_______	☐	☐
_______	☐	☐	_______	☐	☐	_______	☐	☐
_______	☐	☐	_______	☐	☐	_______	☐	☐
Total _______			Total _______			Total _______		

*Debit - Money comes out of your account right away (checking or savings) when you spend it.
*Credit - Purchases add to a running balance you must pay off by the due date to avoid interest.

Your Sneaky Spend Zones

Month________________

Week (circle) 1 2 3 4 5

Food, shopping, and entertainment are the top categories for mindless overspending

Track these weekly (plus any others you think might be draining your money bucket) and see how much more you keep by month's end!

FOOD			SHOPPING			ENTERTAINMENT		
Amount $	Debit*	Credit*	Amount $	Debit	Credit	Amount $	Debit	Credit
______	☐	☐	______	☐	☐	______	☐	☐
______	☐	☐	______	☐	☐	______	☐	☐
______	☐	☐	______	☐	☐	______	☐	☐
______	☐	☐	______	☐	☐	______	☐	☐
______	☐	☐	______	☐	☐	______	☐	☐
______	☐	☐	______	☐	☐	______	☐	☐
______	☐	☐	______	☐	☐	______	☐	☐
______	☐	☐	______	☐	☐	______	☐	☐
______	☐	☐	______	☐	☐	______	☐	☐
______	☐	☐	______	☐	☐	______	☐	☐

Total ________ Total ________ Total ________

*Debit - Money comes out of your account right away (checking or savings) when you spend it.
*Credit - Purchases add to a running balance you must pay off by the due date to avoid interest.

Your Sneaky Spend Zones

Month________________

Week (circle) 1 2 3 4 5

Food, shopping, and entertainment are the top categories for mindless overspending

Track these weekly (plus any others you think might be draining your money bucket) and see how much more you keep by month's end!

FOOD			SHOPPING			ENTERTAINMENT		
Amount $	Debit*	Credit*	Amount $	Debit	Credit	Amount $	Debit	Credit
______	☐	☐	______	☐	☐	______	☐	☐
______	☐	☐	______	☐	☐	______	☐	☐
______	☐	☐	______	☐	☐	______	☐	☐
______	☐	☐	______	☐	☐	______	☐	☐
______	☐	☐	______	☐	☐	______	☐	☐
______	☐	☐	______	☐	☐	______	☐	☐
______	☐	☐	______	☐	☐	______	☐	☐
______	☐	☐	______	☐	☐	______	☐	☐
______	☐	☐	______	☐	☐	______	☐	☐
______	☐	☐	______	☐	☐	______	☐	☐
Total ______			Total ______			Total ______		

*Debit - Money comes out of your account right away (checking or savings) when you spend it.
*Credit - Purchases add to a running balance you must pay off by the due date to avoid interest.

Your Sneaky Spend Zones

Month________________

Week (circle) 1 2 3 4 5

Food, shopping, and entertainment are the top categories for mindless overspending

Track these weekly (plus any others you think might be draining your money bucket) and see how much more you keep by month's end!

FOOD			SHOPPING			ENTERTAINMENT		
Amount $	Debit*	Credit*	Amount $	Debit	Credit	Amount $	Debit	Credit
________	☐	☐	________	☐	☐	________	☐	☐
________	☐	☐	________	☐	☐	________	☐	☐
________	☐	☐	________	☐	☐	________	☐	☐
________	☐	☐	________	☐	☐	________	☐	☐
________	☐	☐	________	☐	☐	________	☐	☐
________	☐	☐	________	☐	☐	________	☐	☐
________	☐	☐	________	☐	☐	________	☐	☐
________	☐	☐	________	☐	☐	________	☐	☐
________	☐	☐	________	☐	☐	________	☐	☐
________	☐	☐	________	☐	☐	________	☐	☐

Total ________ Total ________ Total ________

*Debit - Money comes out of your account right away (checking or savings) when you spend it.
*Credit - Purchases add to a running balance you must pay off by the due date to avoid interest.

Credit Card Spending Tracker

Spend, Pay, Repeat

Payment Date	Card Name	Charged	Paid	Balance Up or Down

Track + Tackle Debt

Tackle Your Debt, One Month at a Time

Use this chart to list your debts, track your minimum and extra payments, and watch your balances shrink. Seeing your progress month by month helps you stay motivated and focused. Every extra dollar brings you one step closer to debt freedom—so keep going!

	LOAN ________	LOAN ________	LOAN ________	LOAN ________	LOAN ________	LOAN ________
Starting Balance						
Minimum Payment						
Extra Payment (Choose one loan to focus on)						
Month ____________						
Month ____________						
Month ____________						
Total Paid						
PAID OFF!						

Snowball vs. Avalanche: What's the Difference?

Both are popular ways to pay off debt - but they use different strategies to keep you motivated:

Debt Snowball

Focus on the smallest balance first

⟶ Make minimum payments on all others

⟶ Throw all extra money at smallest debt

✓ Quick success builds confidence and momentum!

Debt Avalanche

Focus on the highest interest rate first

⟶ Pay minimums on others

⟶ Put all extra toward the highest-interest debt

✓ Saves the most money over time

Refocus, Reflect & Notes

Use this space to capture your thoughts, goals or aha moments:

"All you need is love. But a little chocolate now and then doesn't hurt."

Charles M. Schulz

https://achievefinance.podia.com

Bill Tracker Calendar

Month: ____________________

Monday	Tuesday	Wednesday	Thursday	Friday	Saturday	Sunday	Amount Left over
☐	☐	☐	☐	☐	☐	☐	
☐	☐	☐	☐	☐	☐	☐	
☐	☐	☐	☐	☐	☐	☐	
☐	☐	☐	☐	☐	☐	☐	
☐	☐	☐	☐	☐	☐	☐	

Instructions

1. Enter take-home pay on pay dates
2. Enter bills on due dates
3. Enter other expenses for this month – insurance, holidays, gifts
4. Track left over amount each week
5. Carry over to next week if positive
6. If negative, use money from another category

Monthly Bill Tracker

MONTH ____________________

Fixed - The expenses that don't change from month to month

Fluctuates - Expenses that change from month to month

NET INCOME ____________________

HOUSING

Date	Who Did You Pay	Amount	Fixed	Fluctuates	Account Paid From	Payment Method (Auto, Debit, Credit)	Still Owe? How much? (Balance)
		$	☐	☐			
		$	☐	☐			
		$	☐	☐			
		$	☐	☐			
		$	☐	☐			
		$	☐	☐			
		$	☐	☐			
		$	☐	☐			
		$	☐	☐			
		$	☐	☐			
		$	☐	☐			
		$	☐	☐			
		$	☐	☐			
		$	☐	☐			
	TOTAL	______					

What did you learn about your fixed and fluctating housing spending? ____________________

Where can your money work better for you? ____________________

More efficient money = more for what matters!

TRANSPORTATION

Date	Who Did You Pay	Amount	Fixed	Fluctuates	Account Paid From	Payment Method (Auto, Debit, Credit)	Still Owe? How much? (Balance)
		$	☐	☐			
		$	☐	☐			
		$	☐	☐			
		$	☐	☐			
		$	☐	☐			
		$	☐	☐			
		$	☐	☐			
		$	☐	☐			
		$	☐	☐			
		$	☐	☐			
		$	☐	☐			
		$	☐	☐			
	TOTAL	______					

What did you learn about your fixed and fluctating transportation spending? ____________________

Where can your money work better for you? ____________________

More efficient money = more for what matters!

Monthly Bill Tracker

MONTH ______________________

Fixed - The expenses that don't change from month to month

Fluctuates - Expenses that change from month to month

NET INCOME ____________________

DEBT MINIMUMS - What is needed to keep the debt current

Date	Who Did You Pay	Amount	Fixed	Fluctuates	Account Paid From	Payment Method (Auto, Debit, Credit)	Still Owe? How much? (Balance)
		$	☐	☐			
		$	☐	☐			
		$	☐	☐			
		$	☐	☐			
		$	☐	☐			
		$	☐	☐			
		$	☐	☐			
		$	☐	☐			
		$	☐	☐			
		$	☐	☐			
		$	☐	☐			
		$	☐	☐			
		$	☐	☐			
		$	☐	☐			
	TOTAL						

What did you learn about your fixed and fluctating debt spending? ____________________

Where can your money work better for you? ____________________

More efficient money = more for what matters!

CARE EXPENSES - Personal, Children, Pets

Date	Who Did You Pay	Amount	Fixed	Fluctuates	Account Paid From	Payment Method (Auto, Debit, Credit)	Still Owe? How much? (Balance)
		$	☐	☐			
		$	☐	☐			
		$	☐	☐			
		$	☐	☐			
		$	☐	☐			
		$	☐	☐			
		$	☐	☐			
		$	☐	☐			
		$	☐	☐			
		$	☐	☐			
		$	☐	☐			
		$	☐	☐			
		$	☐	☐			
	TOTAL						

What did you learn about your fixed and fluctating care spending? ____________________

Where can your money work better for you? ____________________

More efficient money = more for what matters!

Your Sneaky Spend Zones

Month________________

Week (circle) 1 2 3 4 5

Food, shopping, and entertainment are the top categories for mindless overspending

Track these weekly (plus any others you think might be draining your money bucket) and see how much more you keep by month's end!

FOOD			SHOPPING			ENTERTAINMENT		
Amount $	Debit*	Credit*	Amount $	Debit	Credit	Amount $	Debit	Credit
______	☐	☐	______	☐	☐	______	☐	☐
______	☐	☐	______	☐	☐	______	☐	☐
______	☐	☐	______	☐	☐	______	☐	☐
______	☐	☐	______	☐	☐	______	☐	☐
______	☐	☐	______	☐	☐	______	☐	☐
______	☐	☐	______	☐	☐	______	☐	☐
______	☐	☐	______	☐	☐	______	☐	☐
______	☐	☐	______	☐	☐	______	☐	☐
______	☐	☐	______	☐	☐	______	☐	☐
______	☐	☐	______	☐	☐	______	☐	☐

Total ______ Total ______ Total ______

*Debit - Money comes out of your account right away (checking or savings) when you spend it.
*Credit - Purchases add to a running balance you must pay off by the due date to avoid interest.

Your Sneaky Spend Zones

Month________________

Week (circle) 1 2 3 4 5

Food, shopping, and entertainment are the top categories for mindless overspending

Track these weekly (plus any others you think might be draining your money bucket) and see how much more you keep by month's end!

FOOD			SHOPPING			ENTERTAINMENT		
Amount $	Debit*	Credit*	Amount $	Debit	Credit	Amount $	Debit	Credit
______	☐	☐	______	☐	☐	______	☐	☐
______	☐	☐	______	☐	☐	______	☐	☐
______	☐	☐	______	☐	☐	______	☐	☐
______	☐	☐	______	☐	☐	______	☐	☐
______	☐	☐	______	☐	☐	______	☐	☐
______	☐	☐	______	☐	☐	______	☐	☐
______	☐	☐	______	☐	☐	______	☐	☐
______	☐	☐	______	☐	☐	______	☐	☐
______	☐	☐	______	☐	☐	______	☐	☐
______	☐	☐	______	☐	☐	______	☐	☐
Total ______			Total ______			Total ______		

*Debit - Money comes out of your account right away (checking or savings) when you spend it.
*Credit - Purchases add to a running balance you must pay off by the due date to avoid interest.

Your Sneaky Spend Zones

Month________________

Week (circle) 1 2 3 4 5

Food, shopping, and entertainment are the top categories for mindless overspending

Track these weekly (plus any others you think might be draining your money bucket) and see how much more you keep by month's end!

FOOD			SHOPPING			ENTERTAINMENT		
Amount $	Debit*	Credit*	Amount $	Debit	Credit	Amount $	Debit	Credit
______	☐	☐	______	☐	☐	______	☐	☐
______	☐	☐	______	☐	☐	______	☐	☐
______	☐	☐	______	☐	☐	______	☐	☐
______	☐	☐	______	☐	☐	______	☐	☐
______	☐	☐	______	☐	☐	______	☐	☐
______	☐	☐	______	☐	☐	______	☐	☐
______	☐	☐	______	☐	☐	______	☐	☐
______	☐	☐	______	☐	☐	______	☐	☐
______	☐	☐	______	☐	☐	______	☐	☐
______	☐	☐	______	☐	☐	______	☐	☐
Total ______			Total ______			Total ______		

*Debit - Money comes out of your account right away (checking or savings) when you spend it.

*Credit - Purchases add to a running balance you must pay off by the due date to avoid interest.

Your Sneaky Spend Zones

Month________________

Week (circle) 1 2 3 4 5

Food, shopping, and entertainment are the top categories for mindless overspending

Track these weekly (plus any others you think might be draining your money bucket) and see how much more you keep by month's end!

FOOD			**SHOPPING**			**ENTERTAINMENT**		
Amount $	Debit*	Credit*	Amount $	Debit	Credit	Amount $	Debit	Credit
______	☐	☐	______	☐	☐	______	☐	☐
______	☐	☐	______	☐	☐	______	☐	☐
______	☐	☐	______	☐	☐	______	☐	☐
______	☐	☐	______	☐	☐	______	☐	☐
______	☐	☐	______	☐	☐	______	☐	☐
______	☐	☐	______	☐	☐	______	☐	☐
______	☐	☐	______	☐	☐	______	☐	☐
______	☐	☐	______	☐	☐	______	☐	☐
______	☐	☐	______	☐	☐	______	☐	☐
______	☐	☐	______	☐	☐	______	☐	☐
Total ______			Total ______			Total ______		

*Debit - Money comes out of your account right away (checking or savings) when you spend it.

*Credit - Purchases add to a running balance you must pay off by the due date to avoid interest.

Credit Card Spending Tracker

Spend, Pay, Repeat

Payment Date	Card Name	Charged	Paid	Balance Up or Down

5 Signs You Need a Financial Plan

1

LIVING PAYCHECK TO PAYCHECK

No savings buffer or leftover cash.

2

NO EMERGENCY FUND

At risk when facing sudden expenses.

3

UNCLEAR RETIREMENT GOALS

Unsure how much you'll need or save.

4

INCREASING DEBT

Bills pile up and overwhelm income.

5

SPENDING WITHOUT TRACKING

No visibility on money flow.

Refocus, Reflect + Notes

Use this space to capture your thoughts, goals or aha moments:

"I can't change the direction of the wind, but I can adjust my sails to always reach my destination."

Jimmy Dean

https://achievefinance.podia.com

Bill Tracker Calendar

Month: ____________________

Monday	Tuesday	Wednesday	Thursday	Friday	Saturday	Sunday	Amount Left over
☐	☐	☐	☐	☐	☐	☐	
☐	☐	☐	☐	☐	☐	☐	
☐	☐	☐	☐	☐	☐	☐	
☐	☐	☐	☐	☐	☐	☐	
☐	☐	☐	☐	☐	☐	☐	

Instructions

1. Enter take-home pay on pay dates
2. Enter bills on due dates
3. Enter other expenses for this month – insurance, holidays, gifts
4. Track left over amount each week
5. Carry over to next week if positive
6. If negative, use money from another category

Monthly Bill Tracker

MONTH ____________________

Fixed - The expenses that don't change from month to month

Fluctuates - Expenses that change from month to month

NET INCOME ____________________

HOUSING

Date	Who Did You Pay	Amount	Fixed	Fluctuates	Account Paid From	Payment Method (Auto, Debit, Credit)	Still Owe? How much? (Balance)
		$	☐	☐			
		$	☐	☐			
		$	☐	☐			
		$	☐	☐			
		$	☐	☐			
		$	☐	☐			
		$	☐	☐			
		$	☐	☐			
		$	☐	☐			
		$	☐	☐			
		$	☐	☐			
		$	☐	☐			
		$	☐	☐			
		$	☐	☐			
	TOTAL	______					

What did you learn about your fixed and fluctating housing spending? ____________________

Where can your money work better for you? ____________________

More efficient money = more for what matters!

TRANSPORTATION

Date	Who Did You Pay	Amount	Fixed	Fluctuates	Account Paid From	Payment Method (Auto, Debit, Credit)	Still Owe? How much? (Balance)
		$	☐	☐			
		$	☐	☐			
		$	☐	☐			
		$	☐	☐			
		$	☐	☐			
		$	☐	☐			
		$	☐	☐			
		$	☐	☐			
		$	☐	☐			
		$	☐	☐			
		$	☐	☐			
		$	☐	☐			
	TOTAL	______					

What did you learn about your fixed and fluctating transportation spending? ____________________

Where can your money work better for you? ____________________

More efficient money = more for what matters!

Monthly Bill Tracker

MONTH ____________________

Fixed - The expenses that don't change from month to month

Fluctuates - Expenses that change from month to month

NET INCOME ____________________

DEBT MINIMUMS - What is needed to keep the debt current

Date	Who Did You Pay	Amount	Fixed	Fluctuates	Account Paid From	Payment Method (Auto, Debit, Credit)	Still Owe? How much? (Balance)
		$	☐	☐			
		$	☐	☐			
		$	☐	☐			
		$	☐	☐			
		$	☐	☐			
		$	☐	☐			
		$	☐	☐			
		$	☐	☐			
		$	☐	☐			
		$	☐	☐			
		$	☐	☐			
		$	☐	☐			
		$	☐	☐			
		$	☐	☐			
	TOTAL	______					

What did you learn about your fixed and fluctating debt spending? ____________________

Where can your money work better for you? ____________________

More efficient money = more for what matters!

CARE EXPENSES - Personal, Children, Pets

Date	Who Did You Pay	Amount	Fixed	Fluctuates	Account Paid From	Payment Method (Auto, Debit, Credit)	Still Owe? How much? (Balance)
		$	☐	☐			
		$	☐	☐			
		$	☐	☐			
		$	☐	☐			
		$	☐	☐			
		$	☐	☐			
		$	☐	☐			
		$	☐	☐			
		$	☐	☐			
		$	☐	☐			
		$	☐	☐			
		$	☐	☐			
		$	☐	☐			
	TOTAL	______					

What did you learn about your fixed and fluctating care spending? ____________________

Where can your money work better for you? ____________________

More efficient money = more for what matters!

Your Sneaky Spend Zones

Month________________

Week (circle) 1 2 3 4 5

Food, shopping, and entertainment are the top categories for mindless overspending

Track these weekly (plus any others you think might be draining your money bucket) and see how much more you keep by month's end!

FOOD			**SHOPPING**			**ENTERTAINMENT**		
Amount $	Debit*	Credit*	Amount $	Debit	Credit	Amount $	Debit	Credit
________	☐	☐	________	☐	☐	________	☐	☐
________	☐	☐	________	☐	☐	________	☐	☐
________	☐	☐	________	☐	☐	________	☐	☐
________	☐	☐	________	☐	☐	________	☐	☐
________	☐	☐	________	☐	☐	________	☐	☐
________	☐	☐	________	☐	☐	________	☐	☐
________	☐	☐	________	☐	☐	________	☐	☐
________	☐	☐	________	☐	☐	________	☐	☐
________	☐	☐	________	☐	☐	________	☐	☐
________	☐	☐	________	☐	☐	________	☐	☐
Total ________			Total ________			Total ________		

*Debit - Money comes out of your account right away (checking or savings) when you spend it.

*Credit - Purchases add to a running balance you must pay off by the due date to avoid interest.

Your Sneaky Spend Zones

Month________________

Week (circle) 1 2 3 4 5

Food, shopping, and entertainment are the top categories for mindless overspending

Track these weekly (plus any others you think might be draining your money bucket) and see how much more you keep by month's end!

FOOD			SHOPPING			ENTERTAINMENT		
Amount $	Debit*	Credit*	Amount $	Debit	Credit	Amount $	Debit	Credit
________	☐	☐	________	☐	☐	________	☐	☐
________	☐	☐	________	☐	☐	________	☐	☐
________	☐	☐	________	☐	☐	________	☐	☐
________	☐	☐	________	☐	☐	________	☐	☐
________	☐	☐	________	☐	☐	________	☐	☐
________	☐	☐	________	☐	☐	________	☐	☐
________	☐	☐	________	☐	☐	________	☐	☐
________	☐	☐	________	☐	☐	________	☐	☐
________	☐	☐	________	☐	☐	________	☐	☐
________	☐	☐	________	☐	☐	________	☐	☐
Total ________			Total ________			Total ________		

*Debit - Money comes out of your account right away (checking or savings) when you spend it.
*Credit - Purchases add to a running balance you must pay off by the due date to avoid interest.

Your Sneaky Spend Zones

Month________________

Week (circle) 1 2 3 4 5

Food, shopping, and entertainment are the top categories for mindless overspending

Track these weekly (plus any others you think might be draining your money bucket) and see how much more you keep by month's end!

FOOD			SHOPPING			ENTERTAINMENT		
Amount $	Debit*	Credit*	Amount $	Debit	Credit	Amount $	Debit	Credit
______	☐	☐	______	☐	☐	______	☐	☐
______	☐	☐	______	☐	☐	______	☐	☐
______	☐	☐	______	☐	☐	______	☐	☐
______	☐	☐	______	☐	☐	______	☐	☐
______	☐	☐	______	☐	☐	______	☐	☐
______	☐	☐	______	☐	☐	______	☐	☐
______	☐	☐	______	☐	☐	______	☐	☐
______	☐	☐	______	☐	☐	______	☐	☐
______	☐	☐	______	☐	☐	______	☐	☐
______	☐	☐	______	☐	☐	______	☐	☐
Total ______			Total ______			Total ______		

*Debit - Money comes out of your account right away (checking or savings) when you spend it.
*Credit - Purchases add to a running balance you must pay off by the due date to avoid interest.

Your Sneaky Spend Zones

Month________________

Week (circle) 1 2 3 4 5

Food, shopping, and entertainment are the top categories for mindless overspending

Track these weekly (plus any others you think might be draining your money bucket) and see how much more you keep by month's end!

FOOD			SHOPPING			ENTERTAINMENT		
Amount $	Debit*	Credit*	Amount $	Debit	Credit	Amount $	Debit	Credit
________	☐	☐	________	☐	☐	________	☐	☐
________	☐	☐	________	☐	☐	________	☐	☐
________	☐	☐	________	☐	☐	________	☐	☐
________	☐	☐	________	☐	☐	________	☐	☐
________	☐	☐	________	☐	☐	________	☐	☐
________	☐	☐	________	☐	☐	________	☐	☐
________	☐	☐	________	☐	☐	________	☐	☐
________	☐	☐	________	☐	☐	________	☐	☐
________	☐	☐	________	☐	☐	________	☐	☐
________	☐	☐	________	☐	☐	________	☐	☐

Total ________ Total ________ Total ________

*Debit - Money comes out of your account right away (checking or savings) when you spend it.
*Credit - Purchases add to a running balance you must pay off by the due date to avoid interest.

Credit Card Spending Tracker

Spend, Pay, Repeat

Payment Date	Card Name	Charged	Paid	Balance Up or Down

Track + Tackle Debt

Tackle Your Debt, One Month at a Time

Use this chart to list your debts, track your minimum and extra payments, and watch your balances shrink. Seeing your progress month by month helps you stay motivated and focused. Every extra dollar brings you one step closer to debt freedom—so keep going!

	LOAN ______	LOAN ______	LOAN ______	LOAN ______	LOAN ______	LOAN ______
Starting Balance						
Minimum Payment						
Extra Payment (Choose one loan to focus on)						
Month ______						
Month ______						
Month ______						
Total Paid						
PAID OFF!						

Snowball vs. Avalanche: What's the Difference?

Both are popular ways to pay off debt - but they use different strategies to keep you motivated:

Debt Snowball

Focus on the smallest balance first

→ Make minimum payments on all others

→ Throw all extra money at smallest debt

✓ Quick success builds confidence and momentum!

Debt Avalanche

Focus on the highest interest rate first

→ Pay minimums on others

→ Put all extra toward the highest-interest debt

✓ Saves the most money over time

Refocus, Reflect & Notes

Use this space to capture your thoughts, goals or aha moments:

"To succeed in life, you need three things: a wishbone, a backbone, and a funny bone."

Reba McEntire

https://achievefinance.podia.com

Bill Tracker Calendar

Month: ____________________

Monday	Tuesday	Wednesday	Thursday	Friday	Saturday	Sunday	Amount Left over
☐	☐	☐	☐	☐	☐	☐	
☐	☐	☐	☐	☐	☐	☐	
☐	☐	☐	☐	☐	☐	☐	
☐	☐	☐	☐	☐	☐	☐	
☐	☐	☐	☐	☐	☐	☐	

Instructions

1. Enter take-home pay on pay dates
2. Enter bills on due dates
3. Enter other expenses for this month – insurance, holidays, gifts
4. Track left over amount each week
5. Carry over to next week if positive
6. If negative, use money from another category

Monthly Bill Tracker

MONTH ____________________

Fixed - The expenses that don't change from month to month

Fluctuates - Expenses that change from month to month

NET INCOME ____________________

HOUSING

Date	Who Did You Pay	Amount	Fixed	Fluctuates	Account Paid From	Payment Method (Auto, Debit, Credit)	Still Owe? How much? (Balance)
		$	☐	☐			
		$	☐	☐			
		$	☐	☐			
		$	☐	☐			
		$	☐	☐			
		$	☐	☐			
		$	☐	☐			
		$	☐	☐			
		$	☐	☐			
		$	☐	☐			
		$	☐	☐			
		$	☐	☐			
		$	☐	☐			
		$	☐	☐			
	TOTAL	______					

What did you learn about your fixed and fluctating housing spending? ____________________

Where can your money work better for you? ____________________

More efficient money = more for what matters!

TRANSPORTATION

Date	Who Did You Pay	Amount	Fixed	Fluctuates	Account Paid From	Payment Method (Auto, Debit, Credit)	Still Owe? How much? (Balance)
		$	☐	☐			
		$	☐	☐			
		$	☐	☐			
		$	☐	☐			
		$	☐	☐			
		$	☐	☐			
		$	☐	☐			
		$	☐	☐			
		$	☐	☐			
		$	☐	☐			
		$	☐	☐			
		$	☐	☐			
	TOTAL	______					

What did you learn about your fixed and fluctating transportation spending? ____________________

Where can your money work better for you? ____________________

More efficient money = more for what matters!

Monthly Bill Tracker

MONTH ____________________

Fixed - The expenses that don't change from month to month

Fluctuates - Expenses that change from month to month

NET INCOME ____________________

DEBT MINIMUMS - What is needed to keep the debt current

Date	Who Did You Pay	Amount	Fixed	Fluctuates	Account Paid From	Payment Method (Auto, Debit, Credit)	Still Owe? How much? (Balance)
		$	☐	☐			
		$	☐	☐			
		$	☐	☐			
		$	☐	☐			
		$	☐	☐			
		$	☐	☐			
		$	☐	☐			
		$	☐	☐			
		$	☐	☐			
		$	☐	☐			
		$	☐	☐			
		$	☐	☐			
		$	☐	☐			
		$	☐	☐			
	TOTAL	______					

What did you learn about your fixed and fluctating debt spending? ____________________

Where can your money work better for you? ____________________

More efficient money = more for what matters!

CARE EXPENSES - Personal, Children, Pets

Date	Who Did You Pay	Amount	Fixed	Fluctuates	Account Paid From	Payment Method (Auto, Debit, Credit)	Still Owe? How much? (Balance)
		$	☐	☐			
		$	☐	☐			
		$	☐	☐			
		$	☐	☐			
		$	☐	☐			
		$	☐	☐			
		$	☐	☐			
		$	☐	☐			
		$	☐	☐			
		$	☐	☐			
		$	☐	☐			
		$	☐	☐			
		$	☐	☐			
	TOTAL	______					

What did you learn about your fixed and fluctating care spending? ____________________

Where can your money work better for you? ____________________

More efficient money = more for what matters!

Your Sneaky Spend Zones

Month________________

Week (circle) 1 2 3 4 5

Food, shopping, and entertainment are the top categories for mindless overspending

Track these weekly (plus any others you think might be draining your money bucket) and see how much more you keep by month's end!

FOOD			**SHOPPING**			**ENTERTAINMENT**		
Amount $	Debit*	Credit*	Amount $	Debit	Credit	Amount $	Debit	Credit
________	☐	☐	________	☐	☐	________	☐	☐
________	☐	☐	________	☐	☐	________	☐	☐
________	☐	☐	________	☐	☐	________	☐	☐
________	☐	☐	________	☐	☐	________	☐	☐
________	☐	☐	________	☐	☐	________	☐	☐
________	☐	☐	________	☐	☐	________	☐	☐
________	☐	☐	________	☐	☐	________	☐	☐
________	☐	☐	________	☐	☐	________	☐	☐
________	☐	☐	________	☐	☐	________	☐	☐
________	☐	☐	________	☐	☐	________	☐	☐
Total ________			Total ________			Total ________		

*Debit - Money comes out of your account right away (checking or savings) when you spend it.
*Credit - Purchases add to a running balance you must pay off by the due date to avoid interest.

Your Sneaky Spend Zones

Month________________

Week (circle) 1 2 3 4 5

Food, shopping, and entertainment are the top categories for mindless overspending

Track these weekly (plus any others you think might be draining your money bucket) and see how much more you keep by month's end!

FOOD			**SHOPPING**			**ENTERTAINMENT**		
Amount $	Debit*	Credit*	Amount $	Debit	Credit	Amount $	Debit	Credit
________	☐	☐	________	☐	☐	________	☐	☐
________	☐	☐	________	☐	☐	________	☐	☐
________	☐	☐	________	☐	☐	________	☐	☐
________	☐	☐	________	☐	☐	________	☐	☐
________	☐	☐	________	☐	☐	________	☐	☐
________	☐	☐	________	☐	☐	________	☐	☐
________	☐	☐	________	☐	☐	________	☐	☐
________	☐	☐	________	☐	☐	________	☐	☐
________	☐	☐	________	☐	☐	________	☐	☐
________	☐	☐	________	☐	☐	________	☐	☐
Total ________			Total ________			Total ________		

*Debit - Money comes out of your account right away (checking or savings) when you spend it.
*Credit - Purchases add to a running balance you must pay off by the due date to avoid interest.

Your Sneaky Spend Zones

Month___________________

Week (circle) 1 2 3 4 5

Food, shopping, and entertainment are the top categories for mindless overspending

Track these weekly (plus any others you think might be draining your money bucket) and see how much more you keep by month's end!

FOOD			SHOPPING			ENTERTAINMENT		
Amount $	Debit*	Credit*	Amount $	Debit	Credit	Amount $	Debit	Credit
______	☐	☐	______	☐	☐	______	☐	☐
______	☐	☐	______	☐	☐	______	☐	☐
______	☐	☐	______	☐	☐	______	☐	☐
______	☐	☐	______	☐	☐	______	☐	☐
______	☐	☐	______	☐	☐	______	☐	☐
______	☐	☐	______	☐	☐	______	☐	☐
______	☐	☐	______	☐	☐	______	☐	☐
______	☐	☐	______	☐	☐	______	☐	☐
______	☐	☐	______	☐	☐	______	☐	☐
______	☐	☐	______	☐	☐	______	☐	☐
Total ______			Total ______			Total ______		

*Debit - Money comes out of your account right away (checking or savings) when you spend it.
*Credit - Purchases add to a running balance you must pay off by the due date to avoid interest.

Your Sneaky Spend Zones

Month________________

Week (circle) 1 2 3 4 5

Food, shopping, and entertainment are the top categories for mindless overspending

Track these weekly (plus any others you think might be draining your money bucket) and see how much more you keep by month's end!

FOOD			SHOPPING			ENTERTAINMENT		
Amount $	Debit*	Credit*	Amount $	Debit	Credit	Amount $	Debit	Credit
________	☐	☐	________	☐	☐	________	☐	☐
________	☐	☐	________	☐	☐	________	☐	☐
________	☐	☐	________	☐	☐	________	☐	☐
________	☐	☐	________	☐	☐	________	☐	☐
________	☐	☐	________	☐	☐	________	☐	☐
________	☐	☐	________	☐	☐	________	☐	☐
________	☐	☐	________	☐	☐	________	☐	☐
________	☐	☐	________	☐	☐	________	☐	☐
________	☐	☐	________	☐	☐	________	☐	☐
________	☐	☐	________	☐	☐	________	☐	☐

Total ________ Total ________ Total ________

*Debit - Money comes out of your account right away (checking or savings) when you spend it.
*Credit - Purchases add to a running balance you must pay off by the due date to avoid interest.

Credit Card Spending Tracker

Spend, Pay, Repeat

Payment Date	Card Name	Charged	Paid	Balance Up or Down

HOW TO SAVE MONEY

FOOD

Make a list and stick to it

Shop the outside aisles of the grocery store

CAR

Keep up with scheduled maintenance

Shop auto insurance yearly

HOUSE

Place utility bills on level pay

Learn basic repairs & maintenance

HEALTH

Get regular checkups

Stay active and healthy

YOUR SAVINGS

Plan Smart. Spend Less.

Save More.

PHONE

Switch to a budget carrier

Buy phones outright

CREDIT

Know interest rate charges

Pay cards off each month

No more than two cards

TAXES

Contribute to tax-advantaged accounts (401k, IRA, HSA, FSA)

Claim all eligible credits

SHOPPING

Set a monthly shopping limit and track spending

Borrow or rent rarely used items

Refocus, Reflect & Notes

Use this space to capture your thoughts, goals or aha moments:

"Money looks better in the bank than on your feet."

Sophia Amoruso

https://achievefinance.podia.com

Bill Tracker Calendar

Month: ____________________

Monday	Tuesday	Wednesday	Thursday	Friday	Saturday	Sunday	Amount Left over
☐	☐	☐	☐	☐	☐	☐	
☐	☐	☐	☐	☐	☐	☐	
☐	☐	☐	☐	☐	☐	☐	
☐	☐	☐	☐	☐	☐	☐	
☐	☐	☐	☐	☐	☐	☐	

Instructions

1. Enter take-home pay on pay dates
2. Enter bills on due dates
3. Enter other expenses for this month – insurance, holidays, gifts
4. Track left over amount each week
5. Carry over to next week if positive
6. If negative, use money from another category

Monthly Bill Tracker

MONTH ______________________

Fixed - The expenses that don't change from month to month

Fluctuates - Expenses that change from month to month

NET INCOME ______________________

HOUSING

Date	Who Did You Pay	Amount	Fixed	Fluctuates	Account Paid From	Payment Method (Auto, Debit, Credit)	Still Owe? How much? (Balance)
		$	☐	☐			
		$	☐	☐			
		$	☐	☐			
		$	☐	☐			
		$	☐	☐			
		$	☐	☐			
		$	☐	☐			
		$	☐	☐			
		$	☐	☐			
		$	☐	☐			
		$	☐	☐			
		$	☐	☐			
		$	☐	☐			
		$	☐	☐			
	TOTAL						

What did you learn about your fixed and fluctating housing spending? ______________________

Where can your money work better for you? ______________________

More efficient money = more for what matters!

TRANSPORTATION

Date	Who Did You Pay	Amount	Fixed	Fluctuates	Account Paid From	Payment Method (Auto, Debit, Credit)	Still Owe? How much? (Balance)
		$	☐	☐			
		$	☐	☐			
		$	☐	☐			
		$	☐	☐			
		$	☐	☐			
		$	☐	☐			
		$	☐	☐			
		$	☐	☐			
		$	☐	☐			
		$	☐	☐			
		$	☐	☐			
		$	☐	☐			
	TOTAL						

What did you learn about your fixed and fluctating transportation spending? ______________________

Where can your money work better for you? ______________________

More efficient money = more for what matters!

Monthly Bill Tracker

MONTH ____________________

Fixed - The expenses that don't change from month to month

Fluctuates - Expenses that change from month to month

NET INCOME ____________________

DEBT MINIMUMS - What is needed to keep the debt current

Date	Who Did You Pay	Amount	Fixed	Fluctuates	Account Paid From	Payment Method (Auto, Debit, Credit)	Still Owe? How much? (Balance)
		$	☐	☐			
		$	☐	☐			
		$	☐	☐			
		$	☐	☐			
		$	☐	☐			
		$	☐	☐			
		$	☐	☐			
		$	☐	☐			
		$	☐	☐			
		$	☐	☐			
		$	☐	☐			
		$	☐	☐			
		$	☐	☐			
		$	☐	☐			
	TOTAL	______					

What did you learn about your fixed and fluctating debt spending? ____________________

Where can your money work better for you? ____________________

More efficient money = more for what matters!

CARE EXPENSES - Personal, Children, Pets

Date	Who Did You Pay	Amount	Fixed	Fluctuates	Account Paid From	Payment Method (Auto, Debit, Credit)	Still Owe? How much? (Balance)
		$	☐	☐			
		$	☐	☐			
		$	☐	☐			
		$	☐	☐			
		$	☐	☐			
		$	☐	☐			
		$	☐	☐			
		$	☐	☐			
		$	☐	☐			
		$	☐	☐			
		$	☐	☐			
		$	☐	☐			
		$	☐	☐			
	TOTAL	______					

What did you learn about your fixed and fluctating care spending? ____________________

Where can your money work better for you? ____________________

More efficient money = more for what matters!

Your Sneaky Spend Zones

Month ____________________

Week (circle) 1 2 3 4 5

Food, shopping, and entertainment are the top categories for mindless overspending

Track these weekly (plus any others you think might be draining your money bucket) and see how much more you keep by month's end!

FOOD			SHOPPING			ENTERTAINMENT		
Amount $	Debit*	Credit*	Amount $	Debit	Credit	Amount $	Debit	Credit
________	☐	☐	________	☐	☐	________	☐	☐
________	☐	☐	________	☐	☐	________	☐	☐
________	☐	☐	________	☐	☐	________	☐	☐
________	☐	☐	________	☐	☐	________	☐	☐
________	☐	☐	________	☐	☐	________	☐	☐
________	☐	☐	________	☐	☐	________	☐	☐
________	☐	☐	________	☐	☐	________	☐	☐
________	☐	☐	________	☐	☐	________	☐	☐
________	☐	☐	________	☐	☐	________	☐	☐
________	☐	☐	________	☐	☐	________	☐	☐
Total ________			Total ________			Total ________		

*Debit - Money comes out of your account right away (checking or savings) when you spend it.
*Credit - Purchases add to a running balance you must pay off by the due date to avoid interest.

Your Sneaky Spend Zones

Month________________

Week (circle) 1 2 3 4 5

Food, shopping, and entertainment are the top categories for mindless overspending

Track these weekly (plus any others you think might be draining your money bucket) and see how much more you keep by month's end!

FOOD			SHOPPING			ENTERTAINMENT		
Amount $	Debit*	Credit*	Amount $	Debit	Credit	Amount $	Debit	Credit
________	☐	☐	________	☐	☐	________	☐	☐
________	☐	☐	________	☐	☐	________	☐	☐
________	☐	☐	________	☐	☐	________	☐	☐
________	☐	☐	________	☐	☐	________	☐	☐
________	☐	☐	________	☐	☐	________	☐	☐
________	☐	☐	________	☐	☐	________	☐	☐
________	☐	☐	________	☐	☐	________	☐	☐
________	☐	☐	________	☐	☐	________	☐	☐
________	☐	☐	________	☐	☐	________	☐	☐
________	☐	☐	________	☐	☐	________	☐	☐
Total ________			Total ________			Total ________		

*Debit - Money comes out of your account right away (checking or savings) when you spend it.
*Credit - Purchases add to a running balance you must pay off by the due date to avoid interest.

Your Sneaky Spend Zones

Month ______________

Week (circle) 1 2 3 4 5

Food, shopping, and entertainment are the top categories for mindless overspending

Track these weekly (plus any others you think might be draining your money bucket) and see how much more you keep by month's end!

FOOD			SHOPPING			ENTERTAINMENT		
Amount $	Debit*	Credit*	Amount $	Debit	Credit	Amount $	Debit	Credit
______	☐	☐	______	☐	☐	______	☐	☐
______	☐	☐	______	☐	☐	______	☐	☐
______	☐	☐	______	☐	☐	______	☐	☐
______	☐	☐	______	☐	☐	______	☐	☐
______	☐	☐	______	☐	☐	______	☐	☐
______	☐	☐	______	☐	☐	______	☐	☐
______	☐	☐	______	☐	☐	______	☐	☐
______	☐	☐	______	☐	☐	______	☐	☐
______	☐	☐	______	☐	☐	______	☐	☐
______	☐	☐	______	☐	☐	______	☐	☐
Total ______			Total ______			Total ______		

*Debit - Money comes out of your account right away (checking or savings) when you spend it.
*Credit - Purchases add to a running balance you must pay off by the due date to avoid interest.

Your Sneaky Spend Zones

Month________________

Week (circle) 1 2 3 4 5

Food, shopping, and entertainment are the top categories for mindless overspending

Track these weekly (plus any others you think might be draining your money bucket) and see how much more you keep by month's end!

FOOD			SHOPPING			ENTERTAINMENT		
Amount $	Debit*	Credit*	Amount $	Debit	Credit	Amount $	Debit	Credit
______	☐	☐	______	☐	☐	______	☐	☐
______	☐	☐	______	☐	☐	______	☐	☐
______	☐	☐	______	☐	☐	______	☐	☐
______	☐	☐	______	☐	☐	______	☐	☐
______	☐	☐	______	☐	☐	______	☐	☐
______	☐	☐	______	☐	☐	______	☐	☐
______	☐	☐	______	☐	☐	______	☐	☐
______	☐	☐	______	☐	☐	______	☐	☐
______	☐	☐	______	☐	☐	______	☐	☐
______	☐	☐	______	☐	☐	______	☐	☐
Total ______			Total ______			Total ______		

*Debit - Money comes out of your account right away (checking or savings) when you spend it.
*Credit - Purchases add to a running balance you must pay off by the due date to avoid interest.

Credit Card Spending Tracker

Spend, Pay, Repeat

Payment Date	Card Name	Charged	Paid	Balance Up or Down

Master Your Digital Envelope System

Simplify budgeting by using three designated accounts for expenses.

Three Essential Accounts

1 **SAVINGS ACCOUNT**

Save for future goals and emergencies.

2 **HOUSEHOLD BILLS**

Cover predictable household bills every month.

3 **SPENDING MONEY ACCOUNT**

Use for everyday purchases and discretionary spending.

Automate the transfers to make it even easier!

Refocus, Reflect & Notes

Use this space to capture your thoughts, goals or aha moments:

"In any given moment we have two options: to step forward into growth or step back into safety."

Abraham Maslow

https://achievefinance.podia.com

Bill Tracker Calendar

Month: ____________________

Monday	Tuesday	Wednesday	Thursday	Friday	Saturday	Sunday	Amount Left over
☐	☐	☐	☐	☐	☐	☐	
☐	☐	☐	☐	☐	☐	☐	
☐	☐	☐	☐	☐	☐	☐	
☐	☐	☐	☐	☐	☐	☐	
☐	☐	☐	☐	☐	☐	☐	

Instructions

1. Enter take-home pay on pay dates
2. Enter bills on due dates
3. Enter other expenses for this month – insurance, holidays, gifts
4. Track left over amount each week
5. Carry over to next week if positive
6. If negative, use money from another category

Monthly Bill Tracker

MONTH ____________________

Fixed - The expenses that don't change from month to month

Fluctuates - Expenses that change from month to month

NET INCOME ____________________

HOUSING

Date	Who Did You Pay	Amount	Fixed	Fluctuates	Account Paid From	Payment Method (Auto, Debit, Credit)	Still Owe? How much? (Balance)
		$	☐	☐			
		$	☐	☐			
		$	☐	☐			
		$	☐	☐			
		$	☐	☐			
		$	☐	☐			
		$	☐	☐			
		$	☐	☐			
		$	☐	☐			
		$	☐	☐			
		$	☐	☐			
		$	☐	☐			
		$	☐	☐			
		$	☐	☐			
	TOTAL	______					

What did you learn about your fixed and fluctating housing spending? ____________________

Where can your money work better for you? ____________________

More efficient money = more for what matters!

TRANSPORTATION

Date	Who Did You Pay	Amount	Fixed	Fluctuates	Account Paid From	Payment Method (Auto, Debit, Credit)	Still Owe? How much? (Balance)
		$	☐	☐			
		$	☐	☐			
		$	☐	☐			
		$	☐	☐			
		$	☐	☐			
		$	☐	☐			
		$	☐	☐			
		$	☐	☐			
		$	☐	☐			
		$	☐	☐			
		$	☐	☐			
		$	☐	☐			
	TOTAL	______					

What did you learn about your fixed and fluctating transportation spending? ____________________

Where can your money work better for you? ____________________

More efficient money = more for what matters!

Monthly Bill Tracker

MONTH ________________________

Fixed - The expenses that don't change from month to month

Fluctuates - Expenses that change from month to month

NET INCOME ____________________

DEBT MINIMUMS - What is needed to keep the debt current

Date	Who Did You Pay	Amount	Fixed	Fluctuates	Account Paid From	Payment Method (Auto, Debit, Credit)	Still Owe? How much? (Balance)
		$	☐	☐			
		$	☐	☐			
		$	☐	☐			
		$	☐	☐			
		$	☐	☐			
		$	☐	☐			
		$	☐	☐			
		$	☐	☐			
		$	☐	☐			
		$	☐	☐			
		$	☐	☐			
		$	☐	☐			
		$	☐	☐			
		$	☐	☐			
	TOTAL	______					

What did you learn about your fixed and fluctating debt spending? ____________________

Where can your money work better for you? ____________________

More efficient money = more for what matters!

CARE EXPENSES - Personal, Children, Pets

Date	Who Did You Pay	Amount	Fixed	Fluctuates	Account Paid From	Payment Method (Auto, Debit, Credit)	Still Owe? How much? (Balance)
		$	☐	☐			
		$	☐	☐			
		$	☐	☐			
		$	☐	☐			
		$	☐	☐			
		$	☐	☐			
		$	☐	☐			
		$	☐	☐			
		$	☐	☐			
		$	☐	☐			
		$	☐	☐			
		$	☐	☐			
		$	☐	☐			
	TOTAL	______					

What did you learn about your fixed and fluctating care spending? ____________________

Where can your money work better for you? ____________________

More efficient money = more for what matters!

Your Sneaky Spend Zones

Month ____________________

Week (circle) 1 2 3 4 5

Food, shopping, and entertainment are the top categories for mindless overspending

Track these weekly (plus any others you think might be draining your money bucket) and see how much more you keep by month's end!

FOOD			SHOPPING			ENTERTAINMENT		
Amount $	Debit*	Credit*	Amount $	Debit	Credit	Amount $	Debit	Credit
________	☐	☐	________	☐	☐	________	☐	☐
________	☐	☐	________	☐	☐	________	☐	☐
________	☐	☐	________	☐	☐	________	☐	☐
________	☐	☐	________	☐	☐	________	☐	☐
________	☐	☐	________	☐	☐	________	☐	☐
________	☐	☐	________	☐	☐	________	☐	☐
________	☐	☐	________	☐	☐	________	☐	☐
________	☐	☐	________	☐	☐	________	☐	☐
________	☐	☐	________	☐	☐	________	☐	☐
________	☐	☐	________	☐	☐	________	☐	☐
Total ________			Total ________			Total ________		

*Debit - Money comes out of your account right away (checking or savings) when you spend it.
*Credit - Purchases add to a running balance you must pay off by the due date to avoid interest.

Your Sneaky Spend Zones

Month_______________

Week (circle) 1 2 3 4 5

Food, shopping, and entertainment are the top categories for mindless overspending

Track these weekly (plus any others you think might be draining your money bucket) and see how much more you keep by month's end!

FOOD			SHOPPING			ENTERTAINMENT		
Amount $	Debit*	Credit*	Amount $	Debit	Credit	Amount $	Debit	Credit
______	☐	☐	______	☐	☐	______	☐	☐
______	☐	☐	______	☐	☐	______	☐	☐
______	☐	☐	______	☐	☐	______	☐	☐
______	☐	☐	______	☐	☐	______	☐	☐
______	☐	☐	______	☐	☐	______	☐	☐
______	☐	☐	______	☐	☐	______	☐	☐
______	☐	☐	______	☐	☐	______	☐	☐
______	☐	☐	______	☐	☐	______	☐	☐
______	☐	☐	______	☐	☐	______	☐	☐
______	☐	☐	______	☐	☐	______	☐	☐
Total ______			Total ______			Total ______		

*Debit - Money comes out of your account right away (checking or savings) when you spend it.
*Credit - Purchases add to a running balance you must pay off by the due date to avoid interest.

Your Sneaky Spend Zones

Month ________________

Week (circle) 1 2 3 4 5

Food, shopping, and entertainment are the top categories for mindless overspending

Track these weekly (plus any others you think might be draining your money bucket) and see how much more you keep by month's end!

FOOD			SHOPPING			ENTERTAINMENT		
Amount $	Debit*	Credit*	Amount $	Debit	Credit	Amount $	Debit	Credit
________	☐	☐	________	☐	☐	________	☐	☐
________	☐	☐	________	☐	☐	________	☐	☐
________	☐	☐	________	☐	☐	________	☐	☐
________	☐	☐	________	☐	☐	________	☐	☐
________	☐	☐	________	☐	☐	________	☐	☐
________	☐	☐	________	☐	☐	________	☐	☐
________	☐	☐	________	☐	☐	________	☐	☐
________	☐	☐	________	☐	☐	________	☐	☐
________	☐	☐	________	☐	☐	________	☐	☐
________	☐	☐	________	☐	☐	________	☐	☐

Total ________ Total ________ Total ________

*Debit - Money comes out of your account right away (checking or savings) when you spend it.
*Credit - Purchases add to a running balance you must pay off by the due date to avoid interest.

Your Sneaky Spend Zones

Month________________

Week (circle) 1 2 3 4 5

Food, shopping, and entertainment are the top categories for mindless overspending

Track these weekly (plus any others you think might be draining your money bucket) and see how much more you keep by month's end!

FOOD			SHOPPING			ENTERTAINMENT		
Amount $	Debit*	Credit*	Amount $	Debit	Credit	Amount $	Debit	Credit
________	☐	☐	________	☐	☐	________	☐	☐
________	☐	☐	________	☐	☐	________	☐	☐
________	☐	☐	________	☐	☐	________	☐	☐
________	☐	☐	________	☐	☐	________	☐	☐
________	☐	☐	________	☐	☐	________	☐	☐
________	☐	☐	________	☐	☐	________	☐	☐
________	☐	☐	________	☐	☐	________	☐	☐
________	☐	☐	________	☐	☐	________	☐	☐
________	☐	☐	________	☐	☐	________	☐	☐
________	☐	☐	________	☐	☐	________	☐	☐
Total ________			Total ________			Total ________		

*Debit - Money comes out of your account right away (checking or savings) when you spend it.
*Credit - Purchases add to a running balance you must pay off by the due date to avoid interest.

Credit Card Spending Tracker

Spend, Pay, Repeat

Payment Date	Card Name	Charged	Paid	Balance Up or Down

Exploring Your Money Beliefs

A journey of self-discovery

Take a moment to pause, breathe, and reflect on your relationship with money. This is a safe space to explore your thoughts and beliefs without judgment. Use the thought bubbles below to dive deep into your subconscious and uncover the hidden narratives that shape your financial decisions.

Consider the Following Questions

What was the first thing you remember learning about money? Where did this belief come from? How does it impact you today?

Complete the sentence: Money is ______. Why do you feel this way? Explore the emotions connected to this belief.

Next Steps

Now that you've explored some of your core money beliefs, consider these next steps:

- **Identify Limiting Beliefs:** Which of your beliefs are holding you back from achieving your financial goals?____
- **Challenge and Reframe:** How can you reframe those limiting beliefs into empowering ones?
____
- **Take Action:** What small steps can you take today to align your actions with your new, empowering beliefs? ____

Refocus, Reflect & Notes

Use this space to capture your thoughts, goals or aha moments:

"The secret of change is to focus all of your energy not on fighting the old, but on building the new."

Socrates

https://achievefinance.podia.com

Bill Tracker Calendar

Month: ____________________

Monday	Tuesday	Wednesday	Thursday	Friday	Saturday	Sunday	Amount Left over
☐	☐	☐	☐	☐	☐	☐	
☐	☐	☐	☐	☐	☐	☐	
☐	☐	☐	☐	☐	☐	☐	
☐	☐	☐	☐	☐	☐	☐	
☐	☐	☐	☐	☐	☐	☐	

Instructions

1. Enter take-home pay on pay dates
2. Enter bills on due dates
3. Enter other expenses for this month – insurance, holidays, gifts
4. Track left over amount each week
5. Carry over to next week if positive
6. If negative, use money from another category

Monthly Bill Tracker MONTH ____________________

Fixed - The expenses that don't change from month to month

Fluctuates - Expenses that change from month to month

NET INCOME ________________

HOUSING

Date	Who Did You Pay	Amount	Fixed	Fluctuates	Account Paid From	Payment Method (Auto, Debit, Credit)	Still Owe? How much? (Balance)
		$	☐	☐			
		$	☐	☐			
		$	☐	☐			
		$	☐	☐			
		$	☐	☐			
		$	☐	☐			
		$	☐	☐			
		$	☐	☐			
		$	☐	☐			
		$	☐	☐			
		$	☐	☐			
		$	☐	☐			
		$	☐	☐			
		$	☐	☐			
	TOTAL	______					

What did you learn about your fixed and fluctating housing spending? ____________________

Where can your money work better for you? ____________________

More efficient money = more for what matters!

TRANSPORTATION

Date	Who Did You Pay	Amount	Fixed	Fluctuates	Account Paid From	Payment Method (Auto, Debit, Credit)	Still Owe? How much? (Balance)
		$	☐	☐			
		$	☐	☐			
		$	☐	☐			
		$	☐	☐			
		$	☐	☐			
		$	☐	☐			
		$	☐	☐			
		$	☐	☐			
		$	☐	☐			
		$	☐	☐			
		$	☐	☐			
		$	☐	☐			
	TOTAL	______					

What did you learn about your fixed and fluctating transportation spending? ____________________

Where can your money work better for you? ____________________

More efficient money = more for what matters!

Monthly Bill Tracker

MONTH ______________________

Fixed - The expenses that don't change from month to month

Fluctuates - Expenses that change from month to month

NET INCOME ______________________

DEBT MINIMUMS - What is needed to keep the debt current

Date	Who Did You Pay	Amount	Fixed	Fluctuates	Account Paid From	Payment Method (Auto, Debit, Credit)	Still Owe? How much? (Balance)
		$	☐	☐			
		$	☐	☐			
		$	☐	☐			
		$	☐	☐			
		$	☐	☐			
		$	☐	☐			
		$	☐	☐			
		$	☐	☐			
		$	☐	☐			
		$	☐	☐			
		$	☐	☐			
		$	☐	☐			
		$	☐	☐			
		$	☐	☐			
	TOTAL	______					

What did you learn about your fixed and fluctating debt spending? ______________________

Where can your money work better for you? ______________________

More efficient money = more for what matters!

CARE EXPENSES - Personal, Children, Pets

Date	Who Did You Pay	Amount	Fixed	Fluctuates	Account Paid From	Payment Method (Auto, Debit, Credit)	Still Owe? How much? (Balance)
		$	☐	☐			
		$	☐	☐			
		$	☐	☐			
		$	☐	☐			
		$	☐	☐			
		$	☐	☐			
		$	☐	☐			
		$	☐	☐			
		$	☐	☐			
		$	☐	☐			
		$	☐	☐			
		$	☐	☐			
		$	☐	☐			
	TOTAL	______					

What did you learn about your fixed and fluctating care spending? ______________________

Where can your money work better for you? ______________________

More efficient money = more for what matters!

Your Sneaky Spend Zones

Month ________________

Week (circle) 1 2 3 4 5

Food, shopping, and entertainment are the top categories for mindless overspending

Track these weekly (plus any others you think might be draining your money bucket) and see how much more you keep by month's end!

FOOD			SHOPPING			ENTERTAINMENT		
Amount $	Debit*	Credit*	Amount $	Debit	Credit	Amount $	Debit	Credit
______	☐	☐	______	☐	☐	______	☐	☐
______	☐	☐	______	☐	☐	______	☐	☐
______	☐	☐	______	☐	☐	______	☐	☐
______	☐	☐	______	☐	☐	______	☐	☐
______	☐	☐	______	☐	☐	______	☐	☐
______	☐	☐	______	☐	☐	______	☐	☐
______	☐	☐	______	☐	☐	______	☐	☐
______	☐	☐	______	☐	☐	______	☐	☐
______	☐	☐	______	☐	☐	______	☐	☐
______	☐	☐	______	☐	☐	______	☐	☐
Total ______			Total ______			Total ______		

*Debit - Money comes out of your account right away (checking or savings) when you spend it.
*Credit - Purchases add to a running balance you must pay off by the due date to avoid interest.

Your Sneaky Spend Zones

Month ____________

Week (circle) 1 2 3 4 5

Food, shopping, and entertainment are the top categories for mindless overspending

Track these weekly (plus any others you think might be draining your money bucket) and see how much more you keep by month's end!

FOOD			SHOPPING			ENTERTAINMENT		
Amount $	Debit*	Credit*	Amount $	Debit	Credit	Amount $	Debit	Credit
______	☐	☐	______	☐	☐	______	☐	☐
______	☐	☐	______	☐	☐	______	☐	☐
______	☐	☐	______	☐	☐	______	☐	☐
______	☐	☐	______	☐	☐	______	☐	☐
______	☐	☐	______	☐	☐	______	☐	☐
______	☐	☐	______	☐	☐	______	☐	☐
______	☐	☐	______	☐	☐	______	☐	☐
______	☐	☐	______	☐	☐	______	☐	☐
______	☐	☐	______	☐	☐	______	☐	☐
______	☐	☐	______	☐	☐	______	☐	☐
Total ______			Total ______			Total ______		

*Debit - Money comes out of your account right away (checking or savings) when you spend it.
*Credit - Purchases add to a running balance you must pay off by the due date to avoid interest.

Your Sneaky Spend Zones

Month____________________

Week (circle) 1 2 3 4 5

Food, shopping, and entertainment are the top categories for mindless overspending

Track these weekly (plus any others you think might be draining your money bucket) and see how much more you keep by month's end!

FOOD			SHOPPING			ENTERTAINMENT		
Amount $	Debit*	Credit*	Amount $	Debit	Credit	Amount $	Debit	Credit
____	☐	☐	____	☐	☐	____	☐	☐
____	☐	☐	____	☐	☐	____	☐	☐
____	☐	☐	____	☐	☐	____	☐	☐
____	☐	☐	____	☐	☐	____	☐	☐
____	☐	☐	____	☐	☐	____	☐	☐
____	☐	☐	____	☐	☐	____	☐	☐
____	☐	☐	____	☐	☐	____	☐	☐
____	☐	☐	____	☐	☐	____	☐	☐
____	☐	☐	____	☐	☐	____	☐	☐
____	☐	☐	____	☐	☐	____	☐	☐
Total ____			Total ____			Total ____		

*Debit - Money comes out of your account right away (checking or savings) when you spend it.
*Credit - Purchases add to a running balance you must pay off by the due date to avoid interest.

Your Sneaky Spend Zones

Month ________________

Week (circle) 1 2 3 4 5

Food, shopping, and entertainment are the top categories for mindless overspending

Track these weekly (plus any others you think might be draining your money bucket) and see how much more you keep by month's end!

FOOD			SHOPPING			ENTERTAINMENT		
Amount $	Debit*	Credit*	Amount $	Debit	Credit	Amount $	Debit	Credit
______	☐	☐	______	☐	☐	______	☐	☐
______	☐	☐	______	☐	☐	______	☐	☐
______	☐	☐	______	☐	☐	______	☐	☐
______	☐	☐	______	☐	☐	______	☐	☐
______	☐	☐	______	☐	☐	______	☐	☐
______	☐	☐	______	☐	☐	______	☐	☐
______	☐	☐	______	☐	☐	______	☐	☐
______	☐	☐	______	☐	☐	______	☐	☐
______	☐	☐	______	☐	☐	______	☐	☐
______	☐	☐	______	☐	☐	______	☐	☐
Total ______			Total ______			Total ______		

*Debit - Money comes out of your account right away (checking or savings) when you spend it.
*Credit - Purchases add to a running balance you must pay off by the due date to avoid interest.

Credit Card Spending Tracker

Spend, Pay, Repeat

Payment Date	Card Name	Charged	Paid	Balance Up or Down

Track + Tackle Debt

Tackle Your Debt, One Month at a Time

Use this chart to list your debts, track your minimum and extra payments, and watch your balances shrink. Seeing your progress month by month helps you stay motivated and focused. Every extra dollar brings you one step closer to debt freedom—so keep going!

	LOAN ______	LOAN ______	LOAN ______	LOAN ______	LOAN ______	LOAN ______
Starting Balance						
Minimum Payment						
Extra Payment (Choose one loan to focus on)						
Month ______						
Month ______						
Month ______						
Total Paid						
PAID OFF!						

Snowball vs. Avalanche: What's the Difference?

Both are popular ways to pay off debt - but they use different strategies to keep you motivated:

Debt Snowball

Focus on the smallest balance first

→ Make minimum payments on all others

→ Throw all extra money at smallest debt

✓ Quick success builds confidence and momentum!

Debt Avalanche

Focus on the highest interest rate first

→ Pay minimums on others

→ Put all extra toward the highest-interest debt

✓ Saves the most money over time

Refocus, Reflect & Notes

Use this space to capture your thoughts, goals or aha moments:

"The road to success is dotted with many tempting parking spaces."

Will Rogers

https://achievefinance.podia.com

Bill Tracker Calendar

Month: ____________________

Monday	Tuesday	Wednesday	Thursday	Friday	Saturday	Sunday	Amount Left over
☐	☐	☐	☐	☐	☐	☐	
☐	☐	☐	☐	☐	☐	☐	
☐	☐	☐	☐	☐	☐	☐	
☐	☐	☐	☐	☐	☐	☐	
☐	☐	☐	☐	☐	☐	☐	

Instructions

1. Enter take-home pay on pay dates
2. Enter bills on due dates
3. Enter other expenses for this month – insurance, holidays, gifts
4. Track left over amount each week
5. Carry over to next week if positive
6. If negative, use money from another category

Monthly Bill Tracker

MONTH ____________________

Fixed - The expenses that don't change from month to month

Fluctuates - Expenses that change from month to month

NET INCOME ____________________

HOUSING

Date	Who Did You Pay	Amount	Fixed	Fluctuates	Account Paid From	Payment Method (Auto, Debit, Credit)	Still Owe? How much? (Balance)
		$	☐	☐			
		$	☐	☐			
		$	☐	☐			
		$	☐	☐			
		$	☐	☐			
		$	☐	☐			
		$	☐	☐			
		$	☐	☐			
		$	☐	☐			
		$	☐	☐			
		$	☐	☐			
		$	☐	☐			
		$	☐	☐			
		$	☐	☐			
	TOTAL						

What did you learn about your fixed and fluctating housing spending? ____________________

Where can your money work better for you? ____________________

More efficient money = more for what matters!

TRANSPORTATION

Date	Who Did You Pay	Amount	Fixed	Fluctuates	Account Paid From	Payment Method (Auto, Debit, Credit)	Still Owe? How much? (Balance)
		$	☐	☐			
		$	☐	☐			
		$	☐	☐			
		$	☐	☐			
		$	☐	☐			
		$	☐	☐			
		$	☐	☐			
		$	☐	☐			
		$	☐	☐			
		$	☐	☐			
		$	☐	☐			
		$	☐	☐			
	TOTAL						

What did you learn about your fixed and fluctating transportation spending? ____________________

Where can your money work better for you? ____________________

More efficient money = more for what matters!

Monthly Bill Tracker

MONTH ______________________

Fixed - The expenses that don't change from month to month

Fluctuates - Expenses that change from month to month

NET INCOME ___________________

DEBT MINIMUMS - What is needed to keep the debt current

Date	Who Did You Pay	Amount	Fixed	Fluctuates	Account Paid From	Payment Method (Auto, Debit, Credit)	Still Owe? How much? (Balance)
		$	☐	☐			
		$	☐	☐			
		$	☐	☐			
		$	☐	☐			
		$	☐	☐			
		$	☐	☐			
		$	☐	☐			
		$	☐	☐			
		$	☐	☐			
		$	☐	☐			
		$	☐	☐			
		$	☐	☐			
		$	☐	☐			
		$	☐	☐			
	TOTAL	______					

What did you learn about your fixed and fluctating debt spending? ______________________

Where can your money work better for you? ______________________

More efficient money = more for what matters!

CARE EXPENSES - Personal, Children, Pets

Date	Who Did You Pay	Amount	Fixed	Fluctuates	Account Paid From	Payment Method (Auto, Debit, Credit)	Still Owe? How much? (Balance)
		$	☐	☐			
		$	☐	☐			
		$	☐	☐			
		$	☐	☐			
		$	☐	☐			
		$	☐	☐			
		$	☐	☐			
		$	☐	☐			
		$	☐	☐			
		$	☐	☐			
		$	☐	☐			
		$	☐	☐			
		$	☐	☐			
	TOTAL	______					

What did you learn about your fixed and fluctating care spending? ______________________

Where can your money work better for you? ______________________

More efficient money = more for what matters!

Your Sneaky Spend Zones

Month________________

Week (circle) 1 2 3 4 5

Food, shopping, and entertainment are the top categories for mindless overspending

Track these weekly (plus any others you think might be draining your money bucket) and see how much more you keep by month's end!

FOOD			SHOPPING			ENTERTAINMENT		
Amount $	Debit*	Credit*	Amount $	Debit	Credit	Amount $	Debit	Credit
______	☐	☐	______	☐	☐	______	☐	☐
______	☐	☐	______	☐	☐	______	☐	☐
______	☐	☐	______	☐	☐	______	☐	☐
______	☐	☐	______	☐	☐	______	☐	☐
______	☐	☐	______	☐	☐	______	☐	☐
______	☐	☐	______	☐	☐	______	☐	☐
______	☐	☐	______	☐	☐	______	☐	☐
______	☐	☐	______	☐	☐	______	☐	☐
______	☐	☐	______	☐	☐	______	☐	☐
______	☐	☐	______	☐	☐	______	☐	☐
Total ______			Total ______			Total ______		

*Debit - Money comes out of your account right away (checking or savings) when you spend it.

*Credit - Purchases add to a running balance you must pay off by the due date to avoid interest.

Your Sneaky Spend Zones

Month________________

Week (circle) 1 2 3 4 5

Food, shopping, and entertainment are the top categories for mindless overspending

Track these weekly (plus any others you think might be draining your money bucket) and see how much more you keep by month's end!

FOOD			SHOPPING			ENTERTAINMENT		
Amount $	Debit*	Credit*	Amount $	Debit	Credit	Amount $	Debit	Credit
______	☐	☐	______	☐	☐	______	☐	☐
______	☐	☐	______	☐	☐	______	☐	☐
______	☐	☐	______	☐	☐	______	☐	☐
______	☐	☐	______	☐	☐	______	☐	☐
______	☐	☐	______	☐	☐	______	☐	☐
______	☐	☐	______	☐	☐	______	☐	☐
______	☐	☐	______	☐	☐	______	☐	☐
______	☐	☐	______	☐	☐	______	☐	☐
______	☐	☐	______	☐	☐	______	☐	☐
______	☐	☐	______	☐	☐	______	☐	☐
Total ______			Total ______			Total ______		

*Debit - Money comes out of your account right away (checking or savings) when you spend it.
*Credit - Purchases add to a running balance you must pay off by the due date to avoid interest.

Your Sneaky Spend Zones

Month________________

Week (circle) 1 2 3 4 5

Food, shopping, and entertainment are the top categories for mindless overspending

Track these weekly (plus any others you think might be draining your money bucket) and see how much more you keep by month's end!

FOOD			SHOPPING			ENTERTAINMENT		
Amount $	Debit*	Credit*	Amount $	Debit	Credit	Amount $	Debit	Credit
______	☐	☐	______	☐	☐	______	☐	☐
______	☐	☐	______	☐	☐	______	☐	☐
______	☐	☐	______	☐	☐	______	☐	☐
______	☐	☐	______	☐	☐	______	☐	☐
______	☐	☐	______	☐	☐	______	☐	☐
______	☐	☐	______	☐	☐	______	☐	☐
______	☐	☐	______	☐	☐	______	☐	☐
______	☐	☐	______	☐	☐	______	☐	☐
______	☐	☐	______	☐	☐	______	☐	☐
______	☐	☐	______	☐	☐	______	☐	☐
Total ______			Total ______			Total ______		

*Debit - Money comes out of your account right away (checking or savings) when you spend it.
*Credit - Purchases add to a running balance you must pay off by the due date to avoid interest.

Your Sneaky Spend Zones

Month________________

Week (circle) 1 2 3 4 5

Food, shopping, and entertainment are the top categories for mindless overspending

Track these weekly (plus any others you think might be draining your money bucket) and see how much more you keep by month's end!

FOOD			SHOPPING			ENTERTAINMENT		
Amount $	Debit*	Credit*	Amount $	Debit	Credit	Amount $	Debit	Credit
_______	☐	☐	_______	☐	☐	_______	☐	☐
_______	☐	☐	_______	☐	☐	_______	☐	☐
_______	☐	☐	_______	☐	☐	_______	☐	☐
_______	☐	☐	_______	☐	☐	_______	☐	☐
_______	☐	☐	_______	☐	☐	_______	☐	☐
_______	☐	☐	_______	☐	☐	_______	☐	☐
_______	☐	☐	_______	☐	☐	_______	☐	☐
_______	☐	☐	_______	☐	☐	_______	☐	☐
_______	☐	☐	_______	☐	☐	_______	☐	☐
_______	☐	☐	_______	☐	☐	_______	☐	☐
Total _______			Total _______			Total _______		

*Debit - Money comes out of your account right away (checking or savings) when you spend it.
*Credit - Purchases add to a running balance you must pay off by the due date to avoid interest.

Credit Card Spending Tracker

Spend, Pay, Repeat

Payment Date	Card Name	Charged	Paid	Balance Up or Down

SMART GOAL PLANNER

Money Management Worksheet

Use this worksheet to set and track your next money goal.

Remember, **SMART** goals are: **Specific**, **Measurable**, **Achievable**, **Relevant**, and **Time-bound**.

Goal Definition

Specific (S): I want to ____

Measurable (M): I will track my progress by ________________________________

Achievable (A):

□ Yes

□ No

□ Not Sure Yet

Relevant (R): This goal matters to me because

____

____

____

Time-bound (T):

Start Date: ____________________

Time-bound (T):

End Date: ____________________

Notes & Action Steps

____

____

____

____

____

Your Sneaky Spend Zones

Month________________

Week (circle) 1 2 3 4 5

Food, shopping, and entertainment are the top categories for mindless overspending

Track these weekly (plus any others you think might be draining your money bucket) and see how much more you keep by month's end!

FOOD			SHOPPING			ENTERTAINMENT		
Amount $	Debit*	Credit*	Amount $	Debit	Credit	Amount $	Debit	Credit
______	☐	☐	______	☐	☐	______	☐	☐
______	☐	☐	______	☐	☐	______	☐	☐
______	☐	☐	______	☐	☐	______	☐	☐
______	☐	☐	______	☐	☐	______	☐	☐
______	☐	☐	______	☐	☐	______	☐	☐
______	☐	☐	______	☐	☐	______	☐	☐
______	☐	☐	______	☐	☐	______	☐	☐
______	☐	☐	______	☐	☐	______	☐	☐
______	☐	☐	______	☐	☐	______	☐	☐
______	☐	☐	______	☐	☐	______	☐	☐
Total ______			Total ______			Total ______		

*Debit - Money comes out of your account right away (checking or savings) when you spend it.
*Credit - Purchases add to a running balance you must pay off by the due date to avoid interest.

Your Sneaky Spend Zones

Month________________

Week (circle) 1 2 3 4 5

Food, shopping, and entertainment are the top categories for mindless overspending

Track these weekly (plus any others you think might be draining your money bucket) and see how much more you keep by month's end!

FOOD			SHOPPING			ENTERTAINMENT		
Amount $	Debit*	Credit*	Amount $	Debit	Credit	Amount $	Debit	Credit
________	☐	☐	________	☐	☐	________	☐	☐
________	☐	☐	________	☐	☐	________	☐	☐
________	☐	☐	________	☐	☐	________	☐	☐
________	☐	☐	________	☐	☐	________	☐	☐
________	☐	☐	________	☐	☐	________	☐	☐
________	☐	☐	________	☐	☐	________	☐	☐
________	☐	☐	________	☐	☐	________	☐	☐
________	☐	☐	________	☐	☐	________	☐	☐
________	☐	☐	________	☐	☐	________	☐	☐
________	☐	☐	________	☐	☐	________	☐	☐

Total ________ Total ________ Total ________

*Debit - Money comes out of your account right away (checking or savings) when you spend it.
*Credit - Purchases add to a running balance you must pay off by the due date to avoid interest.

Your Sneaky Spend Zones

Month________________

Week (circle) 1 2 3 4 5

Food, shopping, and entertainment are the top categories for mindless overspending

Track these weekly (plus any others you think might be draining your money bucket) and see how much more you keep by month's end!

FOOD			SHOPPING			ENTERTAINMENT		
Amount $	Debit*	Credit*	Amount $	Debit	Credit	Amount $	Debit	Credit
______	☐	☐	______	☐	☐	______	☐	☐
______	☐	☐	______	☐	☐	______	☐	☐
______	☐	☐	______	☐	☐	______	☐	☐
______	☐	☐	______	☐	☐	______	☐	☐
______	☐	☐	______	☐	☐	______	☐	☐
______	☐	☐	______	☐	☐	______	☐	☐
______	☐	☐	______	☐	☐	______	☐	☐
______	☐	☐	______	☐	☐	______	☐	☐
______	☐	☐	______	☐	☐	______	☐	☐
______	☐	☐	______	☐	☐	______	☐	☐
Total ______			Total ______			Total ______		

*Debit - Money comes out of your account right away (checking or savings) when you spend it.
*Credit - Purchases add to a running balance you must pay off by the due date to avoid interest.

Your Sneaky Spend Zones

Month________________

Week (circle) 1 2 3 4 5

Food, shopping, and entertainment are the top categories for mindless overspending

Track these weekly (plus any others you think might be draining your money bucket) and see how much more you keep by month's end!

FOOD			SHOPPING			ENTERTAINMENT		
Amount $	Debit*	Credit*	Amount $	Debit	Credit	Amount $	Debit	Credit
______	☐	☐	______	☐	☐	______	☐	☐
______	☐	☐	______	☐	☐	______	☐	☐
______	☐	☐	______	☐	☐	______	☐	☐
______	☐	☐	______	☐	☐	______	☐	☐
______	☐	☐	______	☐	☐	______	☐	☐
______	☐	☐	______	☐	☐	______	☐	☐
______	☐	☐	______	☐	☐	______	☐	☐
______	☐	☐	______	☐	☐	______	☐	☐
______	☐	☐	______	☐	☐	______	☐	☐
______	☐	☐	______	☐	☐	______	☐	☐
Total ______			Total ______			Total ______		

*Debit - Money comes out of your account right away (checking or savings) when you spend it.
*Credit - Purchases add to a running balance you must pay off by the due date to avoid interest.

Refocus, Reflect + Notes

Use this space to capture your thoughts, goals or aha moments:

"You can, you should, and if you're brave enough to start, you will." – Stephen King

https://achievefinance.podia.com

Bill Tracker Calendar

Month: ____________________

Monday	Tuesday	Wednesday	Thursday	Friday	Saturday	Sunday	Amount Left over
☐	☐	☐	☐	☐	☐	☐	
☐	☐	☐	☐	☐	☐	☐	
☐	☐	☐	☐	☐	☐	☐	
☐	☐	☐	☐	☐	☐	☐	
☐	☐	☐	☐	☐	☐	☐	

Instructions

1. Enter take-home pay on pay dates
2. Enter bills on due dates
3. Enter other expenses for this month – insurance, holidays, gifts
4. Track left over amount each week
5. Carry over to next week if positive
6. If negative, use money from another category

Monthly Bill Tracker

MONTH ______________________

Fixed - The expenses that don't change from month to month

Fluctuates - Expenses that change from month to month

NET INCOME ______________________

HOUSING

Date	Who Did You Pay	Amount	Fixed	Fluctuates	Account Paid From	Payment Method (Auto, Debit, Credit)	Still Owe? How much? (Balance)
		$	☐	☐			
		$	☐	☐			
		$	☐	☐			
		$	☐	☐			
		$	☐	☐			
		$	☐	☐			
		$	☐	☐			
		$	☐	☐			
		$	☐	☐			
		$	☐	☐			
		$	☐	☐			
		$	☐	☐			
		$	☐	☐			
		$	☐	☐			
	TOTAL	______					

What did you learn about your fixed and fluctating housing spending? ______________________

Where can your money work better for you? ______________________

More efficient money = more for what matters!

TRANSPORTATION

Date	Who Did You Pay	Amount	Fixed	Fluctuates	Account Paid From	Payment Method (Auto, Debit, Credit)	Still Owe? How much? (Balance)
		$	☐	☐			
		$	☐	☐			
		$	☐	☐			
		$	☐	☐			
		$	☐	☐			
		$	☐	☐			
		$	☐	☐			
		$	☐	☐			
		$	☐	☐			
		$	☐	☐			
		$	☐	☐			
		$	☐	☐			
	TOTAL	______					

What did you learn about your fixed and fluctating transportation spending? ______________________

Where can your money work better for you? ______________________

More efficient money = more for what matters!

Monthly Bill Tracker

MONTH ________________________

Fixed - The expenses that don't change from month to month

Fluctuates - Expenses that change from month to month

NET INCOME ____________________

DEBT MINIMUMS - What is needed to keep the debt current

Date	Who Did You Pay	Amount	Fixed	Fluctuates	Account Paid From	Payment Method (Auto, Debit, Credit)	Still Owe? How much? (Balance)
		$	☐	☐			
		$	☐	☐			
		$	☐	☐			
		$	☐	☐			
		$	☐	☐			
		$	☐	☐			
		$	☐	☐			
		$	☐	☐			
		$	☐	☐			
		$	☐	☐			
		$	☐	☐			
		$	☐	☐			
		$	☐	☐			
		$	☐	☐			
	TOTAL						

What did you learn about your fixed and fluctating debt spending? ____________________

Where can your money work better for you? ____________________

More efficient money = more for what matters!

CARE EXPENSES - Personal, Children, Pets

Date	Who Did You Pay	Amount	Fixed	Fluctuates	Account Paid From	Payment Method (Auto, Debit, Credit)	Still Owe? How much? (Balance)
		$	☐	☐			
		$	☐	☐			
		$	☐	☐			
		$	☐	☐			
		$	☐	☐			
		$	☐	☐			
		$	☐	☐			
		$	☐	☐			
		$	☐	☐			
		$	☐	☐			
		$	☐	☐			
		$	☐	☐			
		$	☐	☐			
	TOTAL						

What did you learn about your fixed and fluctating care spending? ____________________

Where can your money work better for you? ____________________

More efficient money = more for what matters!

Credit Card Spending Tracker

Spend, Pay, Repeat

Payment Date	Card Name	Charged	Paid	Balance Up or Down

MY MONEY MAP

WHAT ONE GOAL IS FIRST?

WHY DO YOU WANT THIS?

TOOLS TO SUCCEED

Where will you track success?

TIME FRAME - WHEN

SUPPORT

Who do you have to cheer you on to the goals? Write their names here.

HOW TO GET THERE

Name 3 steps you can take today to start reaching these goals

Your Sneaky Spend Zones

Month ________________

Week (circle) 1 2 3 4 5

Food, shopping, and entertainment are the top categories for mindless overspending

Track these weekly (plus any others you think might be draining your money bucket) and see how much more you keep by month's end!

FOOD			SHOPPING			ENTERTAINMENT		
Amount $	Debit*	Credit*	Amount $	Debit	Credit	Amount $	Debit	Credit
______	☐	☐	______	☐	☐	______	☐	☐
______	☐	☐	______	☐	☐	______	☐	☐
______	☐	☐	______	☐	☐	______	☐	☐
______	☐	☐	______	☐	☐	______	☐	☐
______	☐	☐	______	☐	☐	______	☐	☐
______	☐	☐	______	☐	☐	______	☐	☐
______	☐	☐	______	☐	☐	______	☐	☐
______	☐	☐	______	☐	☐	______	☐	☐
______	☐	☐	______	☐	☐	______	☐	☐
______	☐	☐	______	☐	☐	______	☐	☐
Total ______			Total ______			Total ______		

*Debit - Money comes out of your account right away (checking or savings) when you spend it.
*Credit - Purchases add to a running balance you must pay off by the due date to avoid interest.

Your Sneaky Spend Zones

Month________________

Week (circle) 1 2 3 4 5

Food, shopping, and entertainment are the top categories for mindless overspending

Track these weekly (plus any others you think might be draining your money bucket) and see how much more you keep by month's end!

FOOD			SHOPPING			ENTERTAINMENT		
Amount $	Debit*	Credit*	Amount $	Debit	Credit	Amount $	Debit	Credit
______	☐	☐	______	☐	☐	______	☐	☐
______	☐	☐	______	☐	☐	______	☐	☐
______	☐	☐	______	☐	☐	______	☐	☐
______	☐	☐	______	☐	☐	______	☐	☐
______	☐	☐	______	☐	☐	______	☐	☐
______	☐	☐	______	☐	☐	______	☐	☐
______	☐	☐	______	☐	☐	______	☐	☐
______	☐	☐	______	☐	☐	______	☐	☐
______	☐	☐	______	☐	☐	______	☐	☐
______	☐	☐	______	☐	☐	______	☐	☐

Total ________ Total ________ Total ________

*Debit - Money comes out of your account right away (checking or savings) when you spend it.
*Credit - Purchases add to a running balance you must pay off by the due date to avoid interest.

Your Sneaky Spend Zones

Month________________

Week (circle) 1 2 3 4 5

Food, shopping, and entertainment are the top categories for mindless overspending

Track these weekly (plus any others you think might be draining your money bucket) and see how much more you keep by month's end!

FOOD			SHOPPING			ENTERTAINMENT		
Amount $	Debit*	Credit*	Amount $	Debit	Credit	Amount $	Debit	Credit
______	☐	☐	______	☐	☐	______	☐	☐
______	☐	☐	______	☐	☐	______	☐	☐
______	☐	☐	______	☐	☐	______	☐	☐
______	☐	☐	______	☐	☐	______	☐	☐
______	☐	☐	______	☐	☐	______	☐	☐
______	☐	☐	______	☐	☐	______	☐	☐
______	☐	☐	______	☐	☐	______	☐	☐
______	☐	☐	______	☐	☐	______	☐	☐
______	☐	☐	______	☐	☐	______	☐	☐
______	☐	☐	______	☐	☐	______	☐	☐
Total ______			Total ______			Total ______		

*Debit - Money comes out of your account right away (checking or savings) when you spend it.
*Credit - Purchases add to a running balance you must pay off by the due date to avoid interest.

Your Sneaky Spend Zones

Month________________

Week (circle) 1 2 3 4 5

Food, shopping, and entertainment are the top categories for mindless overspending

Track these weekly (plus any others you think might be draining your money bucket) and see how much more you keep by month's end!

FOOD			SHOPPING			ENTERTAINMENT		
Amount $	Debit*	Credit*	Amount $	Debit	Credit	Amount $	Debit	Credit
______	☐	☐	______	☐	☐	______	☐	☐
______	☐	☐	______	☐	☐	______	☐	☐
______	☐	☐	______	☐	☐	______	☐	☐
______	☐	☐	______	☐	☐	______	☐	☐
______	☐	☐	______	☐	☐	______	☐	☐
______	☐	☐	______	☐	☐	______	☐	☐
______	☐	☐	______	☐	☐	______	☐	☐
______	☐	☐	______	☐	☐	______	☐	☐
______	☐	☐	______	☐	☐	______	☐	☐
______	☐	☐	______	☐	☐	______	☐	☐
Total ______			Total ______			Total ______		

*Debit - Money comes out of your account right away (checking or savings) when you spend it.

*Credit - Purchases add to a running balance you must pay off by the due date to avoid interest.

The Four H's Change Wheel

A reflection on how your confidence has grown in each area

HANDS- *MONEY BEHAVIORS*

HEAD - *FINANCIAL KNOWLEDGE*

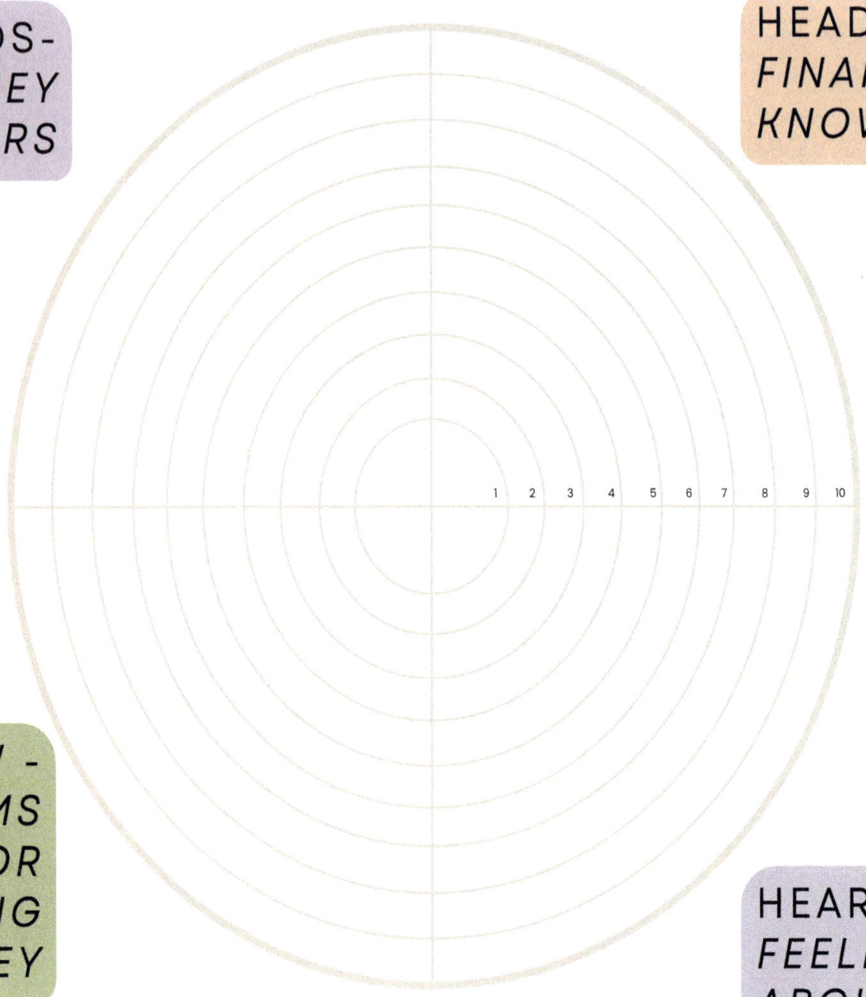

HOW - *SYSTEMS FOR TRACKING MONEY*

HEART - *FEELINGS ABOUT MONEY*

"Look how far you've come - every step counts. Celebrate you."

WHAT I DISCOVERED ABOUT MYSELF...

____

____

____

____

____

____

Your Journal is Just the Beginning

Ready to take the next step to Train Your Money™?

The *Sit, Buck, Sit* course walks you step by step through the exact system in this journal - so you can organize your money, set up habits that stick, and finally feel in control.

Most participants discover **$100-$200 of "hidden" cash flow** their first month - often more than the cost of the course itself. With short video lessons and quick quizzes that reinforce knowledge and habits, this on-demand course makes financial confidence simple, approachable and doable.

Enroll today and start training your money. I'll be with you every step of the way.

See you soon!

Janice

Scan me

https://achievefinance.podia.com

Emergency Savings Tracker

Shade in a square for every $50 you save.

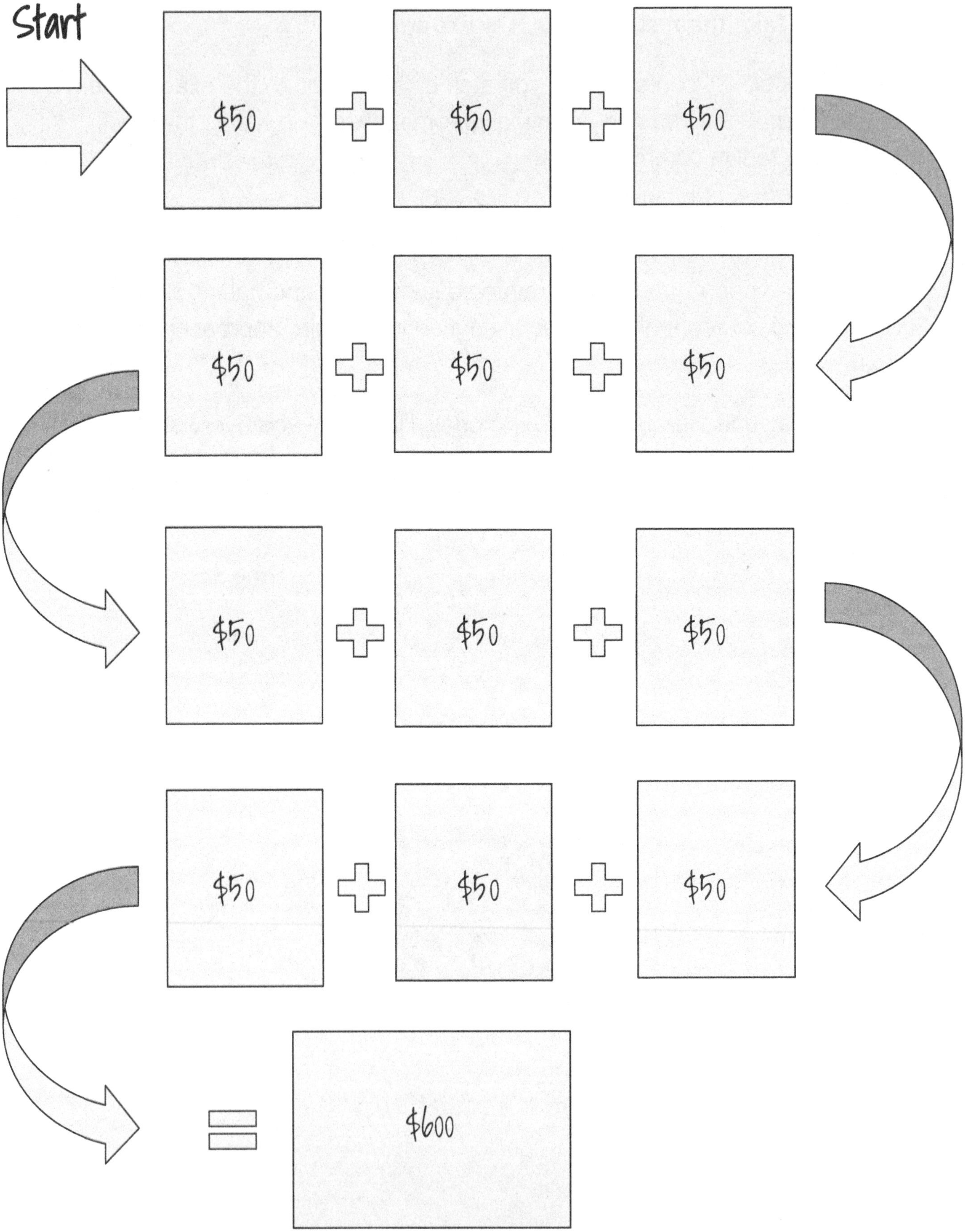

Emergency Savings Tracker

Shade in a square for every $50 you save.

Start

$50 + $50 + $50

$50 + $50 + $50

$50 + $50 + $50

$50 + $50 + $50

= $1,200

Emergency Savings Tracker

Shade in a square for every $50 you save.

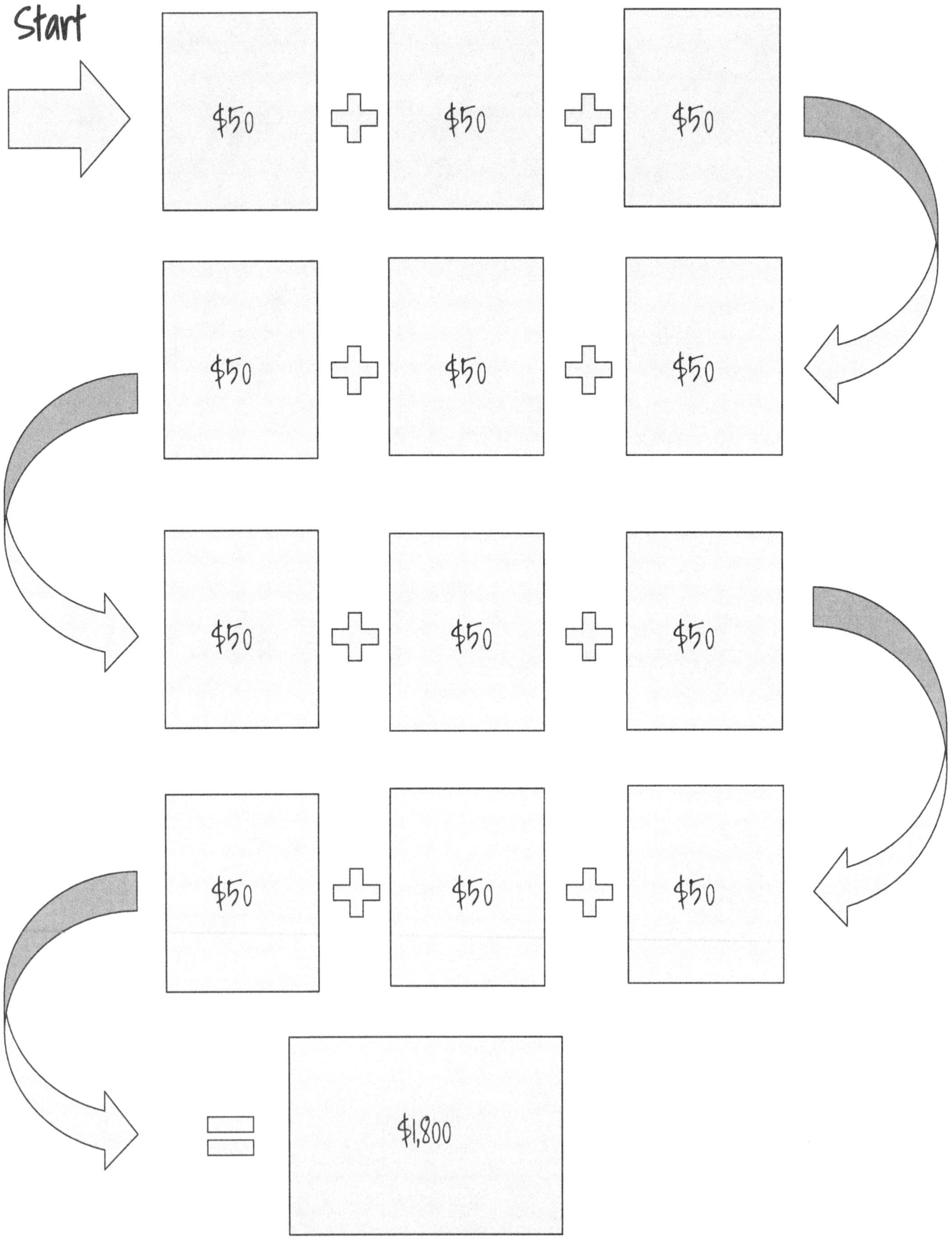

Emergency Savings Tracker

Shade in a square for every $50 you save.

Start

$50 + $50 + $50

$50 + $50 + $50

$50 + $50 + $50

$50 + $50 + $50

= $2,400 Finish

Your Sneaky Spend Zones

Month________________

Week (circle) 1 2 3 4 5

Food, shopping, and entertainment are the top categories for mindless overspending

Track these weekly (plus any others you think might be draining your money bucket) and see how much more you keep by month's end!

FOOD			SHOPPING			ENTERTAINMENT		
Amount $	Debit*	Credit*	Amount $	Debit	Credit	Amount $	Debit	Credit
______	☐	☐	______	☐	☐	______	☐	☐
______	☐	☐	______	☐	☐	______	☐	☐
______	☐	☐	______	☐	☐	______	☐	☐
______	☐	☐	______	☐	☐	______	☐	☐
______	☐	☐	______	☐	☐	______	☐	☐
______	☐	☐	______	☐	☐	______	☐	☐
______	☐	☐	______	☐	☐	______	☐	☐
______	☐	☐	______	☐	☐	______	☐	☐
______	☐	☐	______	☐	☐	______	☐	☐
______	☐	☐	______	☐	☐	______	☐	☐
Total ______			Total ______			Total ______		

*Debit - Money comes out of your account right away (checking or savings) when you spend it.
*Credit - Purchases add to a running balance you must pay off by the due date to avoid interest.

Your Sneaky Spend Zones

Month________________

Week (circle) 1 2 3 4 5

Food, shopping, and entertainment are the top categories for mindless overspending

Track these weekly (plus any others you think might be draining your money bucket) and see how much more you keep by month's end!

FOOD			SHOPPING			ENTERTAINMENT		
Amount $	Debit*	Credit*	Amount $	Debit	Credit	Amount $	Debit	Credit
______	☐	☐	______	☐	☐	______	☐	☐
______	☐	☐	______	☐	☐	______	☐	☐
______	☐	☐	______	☐	☐	______	☐	☐
______	☐	☐	______	☐	☐	______	☐	☐
______	☐	☐	______	☐	☐	______	☐	☐
______	☐	☐	______	☐	☐	______	☐	☐
______	☐	☐	______	☐	☐	______	☐	☐
______	☐	☐	______	☐	☐	______	☐	☐
______	☐	☐	______	☐	☐	______	☐	☐
______	☐	☐	______	☐	☐	______	☐	☐
Total ______			Total ______			Total ______		

*Debit - Money comes out of your account right away (checking or savings) when you spend it.
*Credit - Purchases add to a running balance you must pay off by the due date to avoid interest.

Your Sneaky Spend Zones

Month________________

Week (circle) 1 2 3 4 5

Food, shopping, and entertainment are the top categories for mindless overspending

Track these weekly (plus any others you think might be draining your money bucket) and see how much more you keep by month's end!

FOOD			SHOPPING			ENTERTAINMENT		
Amount $	Debit*	Credit*	Amount $	Debit	Credit	Amount $	Debit	Credit
______	☐	☐	______	☐	☐	______	☐	☐
______	☐	☐	______	☐	☐	______	☐	☐
______	☐	☐	______	☐	☐	______	☐	☐
______	☐	☐	______	☐	☐	______	☐	☐
______	☐	☐	______	☐	☐	______	☐	☐
______	☐	☐	______	☐	☐	______	☐	☐
______	☐	☐	______	☐	☐	______	☐	☐
______	☐	☐	______	☐	☐	______	☐	☐
______	☐	☐	______	☐	☐	______	☐	☐
______	☐	☐	______	☐	☐	______	☐	☐
Total ______			Total ______			Total ______		

*Debit - Money comes out of your account right away (checking or savings) when you spend it.
*Credit - Purchases add to a running balance you must pay off by the due date to avoid interest.

Your Sneaky Spend Zones

Month________________

Week (circle) 1 2 3 4 5

Food, shopping, and entertainment are the top categories for mindless overspending

Track these weekly (plus any others you think might be draining your money bucket) and see how much more you keep by month's end!

FOOD			SHOPPING			ENTERTAINMENT		
Amount $	Debit*	Credit*	Amount $	Debit	Credit	Amount $	Debit	Credit
______	☐	☐	______	☐	☐	______	☐	☐
______	☐	☐	______	☐	☐	______	☐	☐
______	☐	☐	______	☐	☐	______	☐	☐
______	☐	☐	______	☐	☐	______	☐	☐
______	☐	☐	______	☐	☐	______	☐	☐
______	☐	☐	______	☐	☐	______	☐	☐
______	☐	☐	______	☐	☐	______	☐	☐
______	☐	☐	______	☐	☐	______	☐	☐
______	☐	☐	______	☐	☐	______	☐	☐
______	☐	☐	______	☐	☐	______	☐	☐
Total ______			Total ______			Total ______		

*Debit - Money comes out of your account right away (checking or savings) when you spend it.
*Credit - Purchases add to a running balance you must pay off by the due date to avoid interest.

NOTES

NOTES

Janice Pierce, CFP®, RICP® CRPC believes everyone has a money story worth telling - and when we understand our own, we begin to shape a future that feels both resilient and free.

That's why she created the **Train Your Money**™ system: a heart-centered, practical framework designed to take the confusion out of finances and make it feel approachable, empowering, and even inspiring. It breaks down the most important parts of a financial plan into clear, manageable steps.

Maria Romero-Vega is the creative force behind the book's design, bringing its pages to life with clarity and purpose. She played a key role in formatting and preparing the book for publication, ensuring a seamless and professional reading experience. Her eye for detail and dedication to quality made this project possible.

Printed in Dunstable, United Kingdom

91218896R00087